THE GIFFORD LECTURES, 1955

THE PRESENCE OF ETERNITY

HISTORY AND ESCHATOLOGY

THE PRESENCE
OF ETERNITY

HISTORY AND ESCHATOLOGY

The Gifford Lectures 1955

BY

RUDOLF BULTMANN
PROFESSOR EMERITUS OF THEOLOGY
UNIVERSITY OF MARBURG

GREENWOOD PRESS, PUBLISHERS
WESTPORT, CONNECTICUT

Library of Congress Cataloging in Publication Data

Bultmann, Rudolf Karl, 1884-
  The presence of eternity.

  Originally published in Great Britain under title:
History and eschatology.
  Reprint of the ed. published by Harper, New York,
which was issued as the Gifford lectures, 1955.
  Includes indexes.
  1. History (Theology) 2. History--Philosophy.
3. Eschatology. I. Title. II. Series: Gifford
lectures ; 1955.
[BR115.H5B78 1975]   231'.7   75-9540
ISBN 0-8371-8123-2

PREFACE

THE following chapters contain the Gifford Lectures which I was invited to give at the University of Edinburgh from 7th February till 2nd March 1955. The printed text corresponds closely in substance to the lectures as they were delivered. Only minor additions have been made and the number of references to literature increased.

I am conscious that there are many problems which should be discussed further than was possible for me within the framework of these lectures, and I must be content if my attempt to deal with them contributes to such further discussion.

I cannot let these lectures be published without saying how deeply grateful I am for the honour of being invited to give the Gifford Lectures and also for the great hospitality and the manifold and helpful kindness which I experienced during the weeks I spent in Edinburgh.

RUDOLF BULTMANN

ACKNOWLEDGEMENTS

To the Clarendon Press, Oxford, for quotations from *The Idea of History*, by R. G. Collingwood ; to Messrs. Thomas Nelson & Sons, for quotations from the Revised Standard Version of the Bible, copyrighted 1946 and 1952 ; to Oxford University Press, New York, for quotations from *Philosophical Understanding and Religious Truth*, by Erich Frank ; and to the University of Chicago Press for quotations from *The Meaning of History*, by Karl Löwith.

CONTENTS

THE GIFFORD LECTURES, 1955

THE PRESENCE OF ETERNITY

HISTORY AND ESCHATOLOGY

I

THE PROBLEM OF HISTORY AND HISTORICITY

(The Question of the Meaning of History)

Man as subject to History. The Question of Order in Historical Change. Historical Relativism. Nihilism and the Question of how to overcome it.

PHILOSOPHERS today are much engaged with questions about the essence and meaning of History. In English literature we find such significant works as, on the one hand, the volumes of Arnold J. Toynbee's *A Study of History* and, on the other, R. G. Collingwood's *The Idea of History*. One can cite, in addition, Karl Löwith's *Meaning in History*. One of our younger philosophers in Germany, Gerhard Krüger, begins his essay 'Die Geschichte im Denken der Gegenwart' with the statement: 'Today history is our biggest problem'. Why is it so?

The reason is that, in recent years, the historicity of man has attained great prominence — 'historicity' in the sense that man is at the mercy of the course of history, and that in a twofold sense:

(1) It is not, of course, a new conception that the life of the individual is interwoven with the course of historical events. As Erich Frank says: 'The situation in which the individual finds himself is the result of that which he himself, and others before him, have been, and done, and thought, of historical decisions that cannot be

I

revoked. It is only by taking account of this past that man can think and act and be. In this the historicity of his existence consists.'[1] Man cannot choose the place from which he starts. But is it possible for him to set a certain goal at which he wishes to arrive and to choose the way on which he wishes to walk ? Men have at all times been aware that this is possible only to a limited extent. They have comprehended that they are dependent on circumstances, and that the achievement of a plan of life involves a struggle with opposing powers, which are often stronger than man's own virtue. They know that history takes shape not only through the actions of men but also by fate or destiny.

(2) This perception has in our day acquired special urgency in consequence of the events of world-history. Men have become conscious not only of their dependence but also of their helplessness. They have come to feel that they are not only interwoven with the course of history but are also at its mercy. And today this feeling has a peculiar bitterness. For a truth, which is not new as such, has now become clear with frightening distinctness. It is the truth which Goethe expressed in the verse :

Ach, unsre Taten selbst so gut als unsre Leiden,
Sie hemmen unsres Lebens Gang.[2]

The powers which rule as fate over man are not only foreign powers opposed to his will and plans but often such as grow out of his own will and plans. It is not only that 'the curse of the wrong deed ever must beget wrong', as Schiller said, but good intentions and well

[1] Erich Frank, *Philosophical Understanding and Religious Truth* (1945), p. 116.
[2] "Alas our deeds as well as our sufferings, they check the course of our life." Goethe, *Faust*, I.

considered beginnings also have consequences which no one could foresee and lead to deeds which nobody wanted to do. Erich Frank says : 'Man began to recognise that the course of history is marked by the divergence between aim and accomplishment. Man's goal may be set by his own will, yet the results following from his actions do not conform to his intentions.'[1] 'It is a well-known fact that in history the results of our willed actions reach beyond the mark of their intended goal, thus revealing an inner logic of things which overrules the will of man',[2] and he takes as example the French Revolution. It intended a liberal constitution and a federation of free nations, and it led to a military dictatorship and to imperialism ; it intended peace, and it led to war.

Today this is especially clear in the field of technics. Technical attainments are leading to consequences of which their own authors are frightened. Things which were projected and worked out for the improvement of human life threaten by their consequences to damage or even to annihilate mankind. A very simple example is the danger threatening the provision of water in Germany as well as in Switzerland. This arises from the regulation of the river courses as a result of which the level of the subsoil water is sinking, and it is increased by the effluents of chemical works which are poisoning the water of rivers and lakes and even in part the subsoil water. Means for the improvement of traffic and trade lead to damage of human life.[3] I need hardly mention that wars by which a nation intends to make its existence

---

[1] l.c. p. 121.   [2] l.c. p. 137.

[3] Another example with regard to religion and ethics is hinted at by E. Frank (l.c. p. 130). The progress in history toward enlightenment and rationalisation has finally led to a determined revolt against God. 'This development has come about through an inner necessity which the individual seems unable to evade.'

safe can have the contrary result. And now we have learned that peace agreements and treaties may also have unforeseen consequences which bring new disaster in their wake.

The question therefore arises whether our personal existence still has a real meaning when our own deeds do not, so to speak, belong to us. To quote Erich Frank again : 'Man's whole life is a struggle to gain true existence, an effort to achieve substantiality so that he may not have lived in vain and vanish like a shadow'.[1] But this question arises also when we look back into the history of the past. 'History is a sequence of critical actions which bring a new present into existence making that which was present irretrievably past.'[2] This definition envisages history as a permanent process of change, as the rhythm of coming to be and passing away. Is the historicity of man such that he is at the mercy of this change, as a ball in the play of the waves ? Or is it that, though powerless, he is nevertheless a person in himself, feeling himself superior to this change, conscious of having a 'true existence', of verifying it, yes even of gaining it, in the struggle with fate, even in destruction ? As Horace says :

> Si fractus illabatur orbis,
> Impavidum ferient ruinae.

In his speech *De Corona* Demosthenes says of the warriors who fell in the battle of Chaironeia : 'What was the part of gallant men, they all performed. The success was such as the deity dispensed to each.'

This is the subject of *tragedy*, the tragedy of the Greeks

[1] *l.c.* p. 116.
[2] *l.c.* p. 116 ; cf. also his paper 'The Rôle of History in Christian Thought' (*The Duke Divinity School Bulletin*, vol. xiv, no. 3, Nov. 1949), p. 67.

as well as of Shakespeare. Tragedy reveals the true and peculiar essence of man when it shows 'the great gigantic fate', as Schiller said, 'which raises man in crushing man'. In the same sense Pascal wrote in his *Pensées* : '. . . Mais quand l'univers l'écraserait, l'homme serait encore plus noble que ce qui le tue, parcequ'il sait qu'il meurt et l'avantage que l'univers a sur lui ; l'univers n'en sait rien' (347).[1] Again : 'La grandeur de l'homme est grande en ce qu'il se connaît misérable. Un arbre ne se connaît pas misérable. C'est donc être misérable que de se connaître misérable ; mais c'est être grand que de connaître qu'on est misérable' (397).[1]

Even the ancient Greeks saw the world as a sequence of coming to be and passing away, although they were looking not at history but at nature. But for Greek thinking also the question arose about the essence, the 'true existence' of man. And it was answered by the consideration that the change was not subject to chance, but occurred according to laws, and that there was an order into which man fitted well. When man understands the order and his place within it, it is his home. For the law of the order is reason (logos) and the essence of man is also reason, the eternal element in all flux of coming to be and passing away.[2]

This world-view disintegrated in the philosophy or theology of the *Gnostics*. For them the order of the world according to fixed laws appeared as a prison in which the genuine self of man was incarcerated. The genuine self was something beyond the world and its order. When a man perceived the essence of the world and of his genuine self, then he realised his own freedom with regard to the world, and he understood that he

[1] Ed. Brunschvicg.

[2] Cf. also Fr. Gogarten, 'Theologie und Geschichte' (*Zeitschr. für Theologie und Kirche*, 50 (1953), p. 343).

would get rid of the prison when the self left the world at death and rose to the heavenly home.

Shall we say that this is the solution of the problem ? Is it true that man gains his 'true existence' in fleeing from the reality in which he finds himself ? Then the price which he must pay for his consciousness of freedom would at bottom be radical nihilism, a nihilism by which the world man lives in is judged as nothingness. If it is true that it belongs to the essence of man that he is endowed with will and lives responsibly in relationship with his fellows, then the gnostic answer is a great self-delusion. This comes to light in the gnostic anthro-pology according to which man consists not only of body and soul but also of the celestial spark, the genuine self, which is prisoner within soul and body. The gnostic ascribes the whole of the natural and psychical life to body and soul, and nothing therefore remains as a positive content of the self. In consequence the self can be described only in negative terms. Man cannot say what his own genuine self is. Of course, the gnostic may dream that after death he will exist in his genuine being, and he may anticipate this future existence in mystic ecstasies, but even so it remains a negative self. Gnosti-cism is at bottom nothing but a proof of the fact that man is haunted by the question of his genuine self, of his 'true existence' which he cannot realise in the world of change because it is not something objectively demonstrable.

We may ask whether Christianity is able to offer a way out. The man of the Old Testament knows nothing of an order of nature, governed by law, comprehensible in terms of rational thought. But he believes in a God who has created the world and given it into the charge of man as the place for his dwelling and working. Man conceives God as the ruler of history, who directs the historical process to a goal, in accordance with His plan. Therefore he is sure that there is an order in all occurrences, although not one which is intelligible to reason. Certainly human life is weak, fragile, and ephemeral, but the word of God stands unshaken, and man can rely on it. God is indubitable authority, and man has to be obedient, but in this very obedience he is quite safe and secure and gains his 'true existence'.

The Christian Church amalgamated the Greek and the Old Testament traditions. Medieval man feels himself surrounded and supported by the divine order which rules in nature and history. The authority of God meets him in the Church. When he obeys the commandments of the Church he is free. That means : he is able to realise his genuine life, to gain his 'true existence'.

I cannot describe how in the course of the centuries this faith in divine order and in the security of man within it was shaken. The Renaissance, certainly, but also the Reformation, the Enlightenment, and the French Revolution are steps in this process — a process in which the value of the tradition was destroyed and the divine authority, incorporated in it, became questionable and doubtful.

The idea of freedom changed. Freedom was no longer understood as freedom for one's real and genuine being, for realising 'true existence', even in obedience to the eternal order, the obedience which raises man out of the stream of earthly occurrences. Freedom was now understood in a purely formal sense as freedom *from* . . ., namely from the tradition and its authority. The modern striving for freedom began as a striving to become free from the authority of the Church. This did not yet mean freedom from authority as a whole.

Neither in the movement of *Enlightenment* nor in that of *Idealism* was it denied that there are eternal laws in obedience to which man is really free, the laws of the true, the good, and the beautiful. In fact it was the conception of virtue as obedience to these laws which was essential for the Enlightenment. And the conception of autonomy in Idealism is not to be understood as the arbitrary will of the individual who chooses the laws of his actions as he likes. Autonomy means that the free man cannot obey a law prescribed only by tradition, a law which he has to obey blindly without using his own judgment. For that would be heteronomy. The free man can only obey a law that he knows as the law of his own being and to which he freely assents.

But the decisive change in the concept of freedom took place under the influence of natural science and of Romanticism. Modern natural science, stemming from Bacon, Hobbes, Locke, and Hume, and developed in the nineteenth century, acknowledged as real only what can be proved by sense experience and what happens according to physical laws which can be expressed in terms of mathematics. Man himself also became the object of natural science, and therefore the question of his real self, as something distinct from the world of sense experience, was eliminated, and with it went the question about eternal spiritual laws according to which the individual has to live his life in responsibility. Of course, human life is determined by laws, but by natural laws. Therefore man is understood as a natural being, and anthropology becomes biology. Human life is understood as determined by climate and geography and economic conditions.

As a result the concept of the Good changed. The good is only the useful, that which promotes the natural life of the individual as well as that of the community (for the presupposition is that what is useful for the community is likewise useful for the individual). In consequence history is conceived as early as Montesquieu (1689–1755) as natural history. Auguste Comte (1798–1857) believed that history could be raised to the rank of a science by transforming it into sociology. Karl Marx (*Das Kapital*, since 1867) invented 'dialectical materialism' and transformed the Hegelian idea of the objective mind (*Geist*), developing in history, into an economic history. According to this theory, spiritual concepts are illusory 'ideology' born of economic conditions.

The consequence of this was the dissolution of the concept of truth. Bacon and Locke had already drawn the conclusion from the view that all knowledge depends on experience. For if experience changes in the course of time, then knowledge is a daughter of time. That means that knowledge of truth has historical character, it depends on the situation in time.

Historical relativism is primarily the product of Romanticism. *Romanticism* denies that a universal human reason which could conceive truths of absolute timeless value exists at all. Each truth can only claim relative value. So the quest for truth becomes meaningless, and faith in reason as a power in history and as the foundation of thought and knowledge vanishes. It is history which determines the destiny of reason. Later on we shall see how the Hegelian philosophy tries to combine both aspects : the conception of mind (*Geist*) which determines history and at the same time is subject to history. In actual fact the 'historical school', the offspring of Romanticism, did not adopt this philosophy.

In the enlightened eighteenth century the old con-

viction of the constancy of human nature was still maintained. 'Human nature was conceived in terms of substance as something static and permanent, an unvarying
substratum, underlying the course of historical changes
and all human activities. History never repeated itself,
but human nature remained eternally unaltered.'[1] In
fact Hume had already destroyed this conception of
human nature by replacing the concept of mental substance by the concept of mental process. But Hume did
not yet see the consequences for history of this sub-
stitution.[2] It was Herder who broke away from the
concept of the unity of human nature. He distinguished
types of humanity which differ not only in physical but
also in mental characteristics. In fact, he thought that
the individual types were constant, namely, fixed by
nature ; they are products of nature. From this it
follows that human history must be understood as natural
history. Later on we shall have to speak in greater detail
about Herder. Now it is sufficient to say that the ideas
of Herder were elaborated further in the Romantic movement in so far as the individuality of the individual as
well as that of peoples or nations was understood by
analogy with plants, and the historical process was
therefore seen as a process of natural evolution.

To sum up. What is the result of all this ? It seems
to be a consistent *relativism*. The belief in an eternal
order, ruling the life of men, broke down, and with it
the ideas of absolute goodness and absolute truth. All
this is handed over to the historical process which for
its part is understood as a natural process ruled not by
spiritual, but by economic, laws. History begins to
become sociology, and therefore man is no longer under-

[1] R. G. Collingwood, *The Idea of History*, p. 82.
[2] Cf. Collingwood, *l.c.* p. 83.

stood as an autonomous being, but is seen as at the mercy of historical conditions. His historicity does not consist in the fact that he is an individual who passes through history, who experiences history, who meets with history. No, man is nothing but history, for he is, so to speak, not an active being but someone to whom things happen. Man is only a process without 'true existence'. The end, it seems, is *nihilism*.

Can there be a salvation from nihilism ? Can there be a way to detect meaning in history and therewith meaning in historical human life ? Can we detect a law, an order in the course of history ? Today we often hear the call : back to tradition ! But is it possible to renew tradition by a bare decision ? And which is the tradition which we have to choose ? The ancient or the idealistic or the Christian tradition ? Can we close our eyes to the fact that each such tradition is a product of history and therefore has only relative value ? Is it possible to ignore the historicity of man ? Or must we say that the historicity of man is not yet fully understood and must be thought out to its final conclusions in order to banish the conclusion of nihilism ?

Such questions can be answered only when we consider exactly the essence, the idea of history. It seems to me that the very problem is veiled by the one-sided question about meaning in history.

II

THE UNDERSTANDING OF HISTORY IN THE ERA BEFORE CHRIST[1]

The Beginnings of Historiography. Historiography in Graeco-Roman Antiquity. Historiography in the Old Testament.

(1) THE oldest narratives of peoples are not yet history but *myths*. Their themes are not human deeds and experiences but theogonies and cosmogonies, and that means they are really talking about nature, the phenomena and powers of which are personified as Gods. A well-known example is the Babylonian 'Poem on the Creation'.[2] Such myths often belong to worship and rites, whose institution is motivated by mythical narratives. *Mythology* originated in the peoples of prehistoric times and is still alive today in primitive tribes which have no real history. Imagination is still occupied only with observation of nature in its order and regularity as well as in its astonishing and frightening occurrences.

Only when a people becomes a nation through its history does historiography appear. For along with historical experience grows up a historical consciousness.[3] To begin with, of course, the form of the historiography is primitive, being partly poetry, partly prose.

[1] For this chapter I am indebted especially to Ernst Howald, *Vom Geist antiker Geschichtsschreibung* (1944) ; R. G. Collingwood, *The Idea of History* (1949), part I ; Gustav Hölscher, *Geschichtsschreibung in Israel* (1952).—See also Bruno Snell, *Die Entdeckung des Geistes*[3], (1955), pp. 203-17 (where further references to literature are given).

[2] This is quoted by Collingwood, *l.c.* p. 15.

[3] Cf. Fr. K. Schumann, *Gestalt und Geschichte* (1941), p. 32, n. 3.

The memory of important events, of great men and their deeds, is handed down in poetical accounts ('Sagas') such as, for instance, the *Iliad* of Homer or the song of the 'Nibelungen' in Germany, and also in tales which report single memorable events, and stand in transition to historical reports proper. Even Herodotus used such tales as material for his history.[1] In poetical accounts the Gods still play a part, and the same is true of many *chronicles* which recount the deeds of rulers in the form of deeds of Gods. Such historical records, or annals, were kept at the courts of kings and at large temples and also in city archives. They enumerate deeds of the rulers, the construction of buildings and important events such as wars, earthquakes, and other catastrophes. An example from a later time is the famous 'Res gestae Divi Augusti', and many more are found in the inscriptions of Egypt, Babylon, and other parts of the Orient.

May I cite a simple example from a record of the Assyrian King Tiglathpileser I (*ca.* 1100 B.C.) :

I marched on Lebanon, I cut down cedars and ordered them to be conveyed away for the temples of the great Gods, my Lords, Anu and Adad. I marched further on the country of Amurru. I conquered the country of Amurru in its whole area. I received tributes from Byblos, Sidon, Arwad. I sailed in ships of the city of Arwad a distance of three double hours along the shore from the city of Arwad to the city of Zamurri in the country of Amurru. I killed a so-called sea-horse in the midst of the sea.[2]

Another example may be cited from an inscription of the Assyrian King Sennacherib recording his expedition against Jerusalem :

What concerns Hezekiah (king) of Judah who did not

[1] Cf. Karl Reinhardt, 'Herodot's Persergeschichten' in *Von Werken und Formen* (1948).

[2] Gressmann, *Altorientalische Texte zum Alten Testament*[2] (1926), p. 339.

13

submit to my yoke : I laid siege to forty-six of his fortified
cities and innumerable little towns, storming over bole-ways
by assault of battering engines and by infantry attacks . . .
and I conquered them. I took away 200,150 persons, big
and small, men and women, horses, mules, asses, camels,
cows and small cattle innumerable, and I reckoned it as
booty. But as concerns himself (Hezekiah), I enclosed him
in Jerusalem, his residence, like a cage-bird.[1]

Historical narrative proper arises when a people experiences the historical processes by which it is shaped
into a nation or a state.[2] This happened, for example,
in Israel, as a result of the victories over the Philistines,
and in Greece, in consequence of the fights for freedom
against the Persians. Then the stage of chronicle and
'tales' is left behind, the course of history begins to be
presented as a unity, and the historian asks for the causes
and the connection of events and reflects on the powers
moving the events.

(2) In Greece *historiography* became a branch of knowledge, governed by principles derived from typical
Greek attempts to understand the field of history as well
as that of nature. It is characteristic that in the origins
of Greek historiography, in the so-called 'Logographoi',
historical and geographical interests are combined. This
is still evidenced even in Herodotus. Yet the reasons he
gives for his undertaking to describe the history of the
world, so far as it was known to him, are characteristic.
He says that he will publish his account 'lest the deeds
of men should fade in course of time, and the great and
marvellous works which Greeks and Barbarians have
performed should be without glory, and especially for

[1] *l.c.* p. 353.
[2] Cf. Gustav Hölscher, 'Die Anfänge der hebräischen Geschichtsschreibung' (*Sitzungsber. der Heidelberger Akademie der Wissenschaften*,
Philos.-Histor. Klasse 1941, 42, 3. Abh. 1942), p. 101.

what reason they carried on war against each other'. It is true that Herodotus sees the reasons for events in the government of the gods who chastise wrongdoing, humble human pride, and put down overmuch prosperity. But, on the other hand, he also sees the personal motives of the persons and peoples concerned.

Thucydides does not consider divine influence on the course of history and does not apply a moral standard to actions and events, as though there were an immanent law in history according to which punishment follows upon wrong. Under the influence of the Sophists he looks on the human occurrences as natural events and as historian he is, so to speak, a scientist. He endeavours to show the real forces which move the individuals as well as the masses and which set the historical process in motion. The primary force in history is, according to him, the striving for power. While we can say that, according to Herodotus, there is meaning in history in so far as punishment follows wrongdoing, according to Thucydides there is no such meaning. The study of history has meaning in so far as history gives useful instruction for the future by showing how things happen in human life. For the future will be of the same kind as the past.

Thucydides' view of history is typical of the Greek understanding of history in general. Historical movement is understood in the same way as the cosmic movement, in which all change is simply the same thing in new constellations. History, therefore, is not regarded as a peculiar field of life distinct from nature. The Greek historian can, of course, give counsel for the future in so far as it is possible to derive some rules from the observation of history. But his real interest is directed to knowledge of the past. The historian does not reflect on possible future eventualities nor does he regard the present as a time of decision in which man must assume responsibility towards the future. The Greek historian does not raise the question of meaning in history, and consequently a philosophy of history did not arise in Greece.[1]

The historiography of Polybius is of the same kind as that of Thucydides in so far as he also understands history by analogy with nature. He asks for the causes of the historical process, but he does not inquire about its meaning. Perhaps we can say that he conceives the historical process as a natural process in a deeper sense than ever, in so far as he understands history as a uniform organism and therefore attempts to write a uniform history of the world. So to a certain extent he prepared the way for the later Christian world-historiography. The unifying point towards which previous history runs is the Roman Empire. He calls his historiography a pragmatic one, since history is for him essentially political history. He proves the usefulness of history, and likewise the necessity of historiography, by the statement that history is the teacher of the political man : 'The experience which grows out of pragmatic history must be valued as the best education for real life' (I, 35, 9).

According to Livy, too, historiography has education as its aim, as well as the preserving of noble deeds in the memory of the future. In his preface he says : 'We can gain from history standards for ourselves and for our country, but no less can we learn what are the things to be avoided because they are ugly in growing as well as in being successful'. Livy writes critically, looking at the moral corruption of his time, and intends to help

[1] Cf. Karl Löwith, *Meaning in History* (1949), pp. 4-9.

to show how it may be cured. Therefore he tries to prove that a moral law is at work in history, and narrates the events according to a moral standard, presenting the characters of the great Roman personalities as models.

Tacitus also stresses the moral importance of historiography. He says that it is a *praecipuum munus* (a main purpose) of his account that merit shall not remain silent and that he may hold the threat of an infamous posterity over evil words and actions (*Ann.* III, 65). From this originates his psychological interest in the persons whom he describes. His picture is determined by sympathy and antipathy, and his eye is directed chiefly to the vices of his characters. The main vice which poisons the state is striving for position, which expresses itself in ambition, jealousy, envy, and illusion.

In our context we do not need to deal with the method of Graeco-Roman historiography. Our intention is only to show the general trends in the historians. And to sum up, we can say that the task of historiography was understood from analogy with the task of natural science. Connected with this is the fact, as I have already said, that history is not seen as the field of human responsibility for the future. And I must add that the process of history is not regarded as a process in which individuals as well as peoples or nations receive their character by their actions and experiences. The idea of evolution in every form is far from the thoughts of these historians. Collingwood calls this fact the 'substantialism' of the Graeco-Roman historiography. This means that the historical agent is regarded as an unchanging substance in relation to which his actions are accident. The agent from whom the actions flow, 'being a substance, is eternal and unchanging and consequently stands

outside history'.[1] That indicates that man is not understood in his historicity. But about this question we will
speak in the seventh lecture.

(3) The conception of history and therefore the
character of historiography *in ancient Israel* is a completely different one. First, there are no picturesque de-
scriptions of countries and peoples of the kind which the
Greeks, as seafaring men and traders, liked. Then, the
centre of history is seen not in politics but in the actual
experiences and deeds of men of the Israelite people, a
people which is thought of not as a state in the Greek
sense but as a community of men who are neighbours
to each other. The main point, however, is that the
experiences of men are understood as divine ordinances,
as blessings or punishments of God, and their deeds as
obedience or disobedience to the commandments of God.
Israelite historiography is, therefore, not science in the
Greek sense. It is interested not in knowledge of the
immanent powers working in history but in the intention
and plan of God who as creator is also the ruler of
history, and leads it to a goal. As a result the idea of
the organisation of history grew up. History as a whole
is understood as articulated in periods or epochs which
each have their importance for the whole structure. The
meaning in history lies in the divine education or in the
direction to the goal. If there is an interest in knowledge,
it is in self-knowledge, and the historian calls his people
to self-knowledge in reminding them of the deeds of
God in the past and of the conduct of the people. This
call is at the same time a call to responsibility in face of the
future which will bring welfare or destruction, the blessing of God or chastisement. Therefore historiography
is not a means of education for politicians but a sermon

[1] *l.c.* p. 43.

18

to the people. Looking back into the past means critically examining the past in order to warn the present.[1]

This understanding of history develops in the course
of Israel's own history. The earliest historical documents,
the so-called *Jahwist* and *Elohist*, have similarities to
Herodotus in their manner of recounting events, and
are still largely a series of tales. But there is some
endeavour to understand history as a unity, and the course
of events as a way to a goal. The leading thought of
the *Jahwist* is that of the national unity of the people
under the leadership of Judah. This unity finds its
expression in the fact that the beginning and the end
are connected through the divine promise. For although
the *Jahwist* ends his account with the fall of the house of
David and the decay of the unity of the twelve tribes,
still there remains the ideal of the future which will
restore that unity under the leadership of Judah and its
kings.

In the *Elohistic* tradition the history of Israel is also
understood as a meaningful unity. The course of history
stands under the divine promises which aim at the rule
of David over Israel. The narrative of the *Elohist*
derived its principles from the great prophets of the
eighth and seventh centuries. History shows the alter-
nation of divine grace and the nation's sin, of divine
judgment, human penitence, and divine forgiveness.
The narrative displays a certain similarity to Herodotus
in so far as here also the law of the sequence of human
wrongdoing and divine punishment rules the course of
events. But the difference is clear. Firstly, the wrongdoing, according to the *Elohist*, consists not only in
moral trespasses but above all in the sin against God of

[1] Cf. my paper 'History and Eschatology in the New Testament',
New Testament Studies, vol. I (1954), p. 5 f.

apostasy from the right worship which he has commanded. Secondly, according to Herodotus the law of retaliation rules in the essentially unchanging course of history, whereas according to the *Elohist* the course of history goes on its way to the goal, and therefore the divine punishment has the significance of bringing the people nearer to that goal. The *Elohist* ends his record with the catastrophe of the destruction of Jerusalem and the fall of Judah. This catastrophe is understood as the divine chastisement, but at the same time it opens a door of hope for the future, because the dynasty of David is not exterminated.

The Deuteronomic redaction of the history of Israel is also influenced by the prophets. The whole of history reveals the rule of God who has chosen Israel to be his people. Reflection on the past brings to light a permanent cycle of apostasy to idolatry and the divine punishment of defeat and subjugation to foreign rulers, of conversion to God and deliverance. In this way the narrative is the critical account of the past and an exhortation for the present. To the exhortation is joined the promise of a future of salvation for a chastised people, if the people is now willing to obey the will of God.

Similarly in the *Priestly narrative* the reign of God in the history of the past is pointed out and his promise for the future is proclaimed. The interest, however, is not so much in criticising the past as in showing the divine revelation within it. The past is divided up according to the stages of the gradually unfolding revelation. The first three periods begin with Adam, Noah, and Abraham, and are followed by the revelation to Moses. The priestly legislation is dated back to the time of Moses. The goal of this history is the return of the people from exile and their reconstruction as a worshipping community under the law.

In all these presentations history is conceived as a unity full of meaning. Its course runs according to the plan of God. He will guide his people into a prosperous future and he carries out his plan in spite of the obstinacy of the nation. Even after the national catastrophe his promise remains unshakable. Reflection on the past confirms the divine promise, for such reflection shows that the promise was not fulfilled because of the nation's sin. With the promise is therefore always combined a warning, a call to the present to assume responsibility in facing the future. For God will fulfil his promise only for an obedient people.

To sum up. In the Old Testament history is understood as a unity, but not by analogy with nature, and not, therefore, as ruled by immanent laws which could be detected by psychological research. Its unity is constituted by its meaning, the guidance or education of the people by God. His plan gives a direction to the course of history through his enduring conflict with men. From the fact of this conflict a problem arises. If it depends on the obedience of men whether the goal of history can be attained, then how can the divine promise be granted ? This problem cannot be answered, because the future state of welfare in the Old Testament is thought of as welfare within this world. Only the later eschatology of Jewish apocalyptic can give an answer, and this answer appears in the Old Testament only at a very few points (Is. xxiv-xxvii ; Daniel). With this is connected the fact that the subject of history is the people, the nation. Individuals are considered only in so far as they are members of the people. If the promise is fulfilled, then the future welfare will be the welfare of the people and naturally of the individuals as members of the people — but only those who are alive at the time. What then of the others who are already dead ? To this question also the apocalyptic eschatology will give an answer.

III

THE UNDERSTANDING OF HISTORY
FROM THE STANDPOINT OF
ESCHATOLOGY

Cosmic and Historical Eschatology. History and Eschatology in Judaism. History and Eschatology in Primitive Christianity.

(1) ESCHATOLOGY is the doctrine of the 'last things' or, more accurately, of the occurrences with which our known world comes to its end. It is the doctrine of the end of the world, of its destruction.

Myths about the end of the world are found among many peoples — of the destruction of the world by water or fire or by some other catastrophe. It may be left undecided whether all these myths spring from the same kind of thinking, and whether natural catastrophes created in primitive peoples the impression of the end of the world. The eschatology which had decisive importance for the history of the West developed from the concept of *the periodicity of the course of worldly events.* This idea is undoubtedly reached by conceiving the course of the world on the analogy of the annual periodicity of nature : as the seasons of the year follow each other, so do the corresponding periods in the course of the world, comprising the so-called 'year of the world' or 'the great world-year'. Probably this transference by analogy arises out of the astronomical discovery that the place of the sunrise alters from year to year until, having rounded the ecliptic, it returns to its original position. When this round is finished the end of the great world-year is reached. But, just as a new year follows upon the old, as the seasons go round, so a new world-year will follow, and all the events of the old year will return again. The course of time is not a constant progression but is cyclical.[1]

The idea of the return of all things, which grew out of oriental astronomy, was developed in Greek Philosophy especially by the Stoic thinkers. They evolved the doctrine of universal conflagration (ἐκπύρωσις) which leads the world back into Zeus, out of whom it radiates again as a new world. Chrysippus says : 'Socrates and Plato will exist again and every man with his friends and his fellow citizens ; he will suffer the same and do the same. Every city, every village and field will grow again. And this restoration will not happen once, but the same will return without limit and end'.[2]

According to these philosophers, states Augustine, 'the same periods and events in time are repeated : as if the philosopher Plato for instance, having taught in the school of Athens which is called the Academy, so, numberless ages before, at long but definite intervals, this same Plato and the same school and the same disciples existed and will also exist repeatedly during the countless cycles that are yet to be' (de civitate Dei, XII, 13).

This cosmic mythology was *rationalised* by Greek science. The Stoic doctrine of universal conflagration

[1] A. W. Bousset and H. Gressmann, *Die Religion des Judentums im späthellenistischen Zeitalter* (1926), p. 502 s. ; W. Staerk, *Die Erlösererwartung in den östlichen Religionen* (1938), pp. 158-80.

[2] *Stoicorum veterum fragmenta* (ed. H. v. Arnim), II, 190, 16 ss.—Cf. E. Frank, *Philos. Understanding and Religious Truth*, pp. 67 s. and 82 s. ; K. Löwith, *Meaning in History*, p. 248, n. 15.

was founded on a theory of the essence of the elements of which the world consists, and of their mutual interaction. Those Stoic thinkers retained the traditional view about the periods of the world ; but Heraclitus seems to have rationalised it in a more radical manner. For, instead of dividing the course of the world into periods following each other in time, he conceived the world-process as a rhythm of coming to be and passing away, in accordance with fixed laws ; that is, as a constant flux which goes on all the time.[1]

This cosmic mythology was also *historicised*.

The course of the world-year was originally conceived as a purely natural process in which the periods followed each other like the seasons. But later the periods were distinguished by the character of the human generations living in them. The idea of the withering and passing away of every natural growth was transmuted into the idea of degeneration, of the permanent deterioration of humanity, pictured in the well-known form of the successive eras — golden, silver, bronze, and iron.[2] This characterisation in terms of metals originates in the Babylonian tradition according to which each era is ruled by an astral deity who is combined with a metal. On this idea depends the allegorical picture of the empires in the statue which Nebuchadnezzar sees in his dream : the head is golden, the body and the arms are silver, the abdomen and the hips are brazen, the shanks are iron, the feet of iron and clay (Daniel ii). Here the historicising process is carried out still more radically in that the periods are not periods of a mythical past but empires in history : the kingdoms of the

[1] Cf. Karl Reinhardt, 'Heraklits Lehre vom Feuer,' *Hermes*, vol. 77 (1942), pp. 1-27.
[2] Hesiod, *Works and Days*, pp. 109 ff. ; he has inserted the heroic era.

Babylonians, the Medes, the Persians, and the Greeks (or the Diadochi). The historicising in Daniel vii goes still further, for not only are the four empires pictured as four beasts, but the story of the last empire, that of the Seleucids, with its kings from Alexander to Seleucus IV or Antiochus is sketched. *In Iranian mythology*, on the other hand, the historicising remains on the same level as that of Hesiod. Ahuramazda shows to Zarathustra the root of a tree which has four branches, one of gold, one of silver, one of steel, and one of a mixture of steel and iron, and he explains these as the four degenerating periods of the next millennium.

Still greater importance must be ascribed to another modification of the myth which is also a historicising of it. This variation abandons the idea of the eternal cyclical movement of world-years but retains the idea of the periodicity of the course of time. The new beginning which is to follow the end of the old world-era is understood as the beginning of a time of unending welfare. Here the cosmic world-year is reduced to the history of the world.

A sign of this is the usage of the Greek word, ἀποκατάστασις (restoration). In astrological literature it refers to the periodical return of a star to its starting-point, and consequently the Stoic philosophers use the word for the return of the Cosmos at the end of a world-year to the origin from which a new world-year starts. But in the Acts of the Apostles (iii. 21) and in later Christian language, following Origen, ἀποκατάστασις became a technical term of eschatology.[1]

This historicising had already taken place *in Iranian speculation*. Here the doctrine of periods was taken over

[1] *Hermès Trismégiste* (ed. A. D. Nock and A.-J. Festugière), VIII, 4 ; XI, 2. Cf. the notes 17, p. 90, and 6, pp. 155-7.

from the Babylonians, but the idea of the cyclical course of time was abandoned. At the end of the course of the periods there begins the time of unending welfare. Here we may speak of eschatology in the real sense, for here indeed the 'last things' happen with the end of the present world and the beginning of the new and endless world.

Whereas in Hesiod there is no expectation of the last things, in Virgil they are the content of the prediction in the famous Fourth Eclogue : Now the last period of the course of the old world is present, the rule of Apollo. The change of eras is at hand. Now the golden era will return, bringing with it peace and welfare with the birth of the child who will initiate a new human generation.

Similarly in Daniel : Both the stone which, according to Daniel ii, destroys the statue, and also the 'Man' whose reign, according to Daniel vii, will follow the kingdoms of the four beasts, are the 'kingdom of the Saints of the most High', the people of Israel, in the coming time of salvation. Now — and this is of the greatest importance — over against the time of salvation the whole previous history of the world is seen as a unity. In spite of its periods it is undifferentiated in that it is all a time of evil. So two times or two epochs of the world are opposed to each other as the two 'Aeons', the present Aeon and the coming Aeon. This dualism is developed in Jewish apocalyptic thought.

We must remember that apart from Daniel *Old Testament prophecy* had not yet arrived at this idea. It is true that some scholars speak of an Old Testament eschatology. But in the Old Testament there is no eschatology in the true sense of a doctrine of the end of the world and a succeeding time of salvation. Indeed, this dualistic conception is contradictory to the Old Testament idea of God as creator. It is true that Old Testament prophecy contains predictions of salvation and of doom, but they are related to Israel or to its enemies. It is also true that Old Testament prophecy announces a divine judgment but not a judgment of the whole world. It is a judgment within history. Admittedly this judgment is often depicted with mythological features such as cosmic catastrophes, earthquakes, conflagrations, and so on. But these are only ornamental, and are indeed evidence of the historicising of cosmology. The conception of God as creator prevented the idea of the cyclic movement of world-ages from being accepted by Israel, although the imagery of this mythology was to some extent adopted.

This imagery appears in such themes as the prophetic portrayals of the tribulations which precede the change in Israel's fortunes, tribulations which later in the apocalyptic writings are signs of the coming end, the 'birth-pangs of the Messiah'. It may be that such imagery is derived from that of the last period of the world-year. But the thought is historicised in that the time of tribulation is the time of warfare which Israel has to suffer, and also a punishment on the sinful nation. The pictures of the time of salvation may also be influenced by the mythological idea of the returning golden era, *e.g.* the picture of peace between men and beasts (Is. xi. 6 f.), the change of the desert into a paradise, the new heaven, and the new earth. But these pictures are also historicised, for they describe the welfare of the people of Israel. The messianic hope in particular may have its origin in the cosmic mythology according to which every world-period is ruled by a new ruler, *i.e.* a new star. But, clearly, the hope is historicised, for the ruler expected for the time of salvation is to be a king of the house of David.

The poetry of the Psalms has also taken over some themes from this cosmology. This appears to be so in the case of the New Year Festival as the festival of God's accession to the throne. And indeed, this originally cosmological festival was already historicised in Babylon in that the renewal of the world and the beginning of the world were both celebrated as the king's accession to the throne.

(2) *In later Judaism* cosmology was historicised by substituting the destiny of humanity for that of the world. The end of the old world is to be brought about by the divine judgment. The idea of the two Aeons has replaced the conception of cyclical periods, and with this a real eschatology is established. But now, conversely, history is understood from the point of view of eschatology, which is a decisive change from the Old Testament conception.

The divine judgment, which brings the old Aeon to an end, is no longer understood as an historical crisis brought about by God, but as a purely supranatural event, realised by a cosmic catastrophe. The cosmic subjects which were only ornamental in Old Testament prophecy now became important in themselves. All signs of degeneration, formerly characteristics of the last world-period, are now signs of the definite end of the world. The apocalyptic literature expects such signs, and interprets frightening events in nature as well as war, famine, and epidemics as signs of the end. The original character of the events of the end as events in nature reappears, and with the picture of disordered nature is combined that of the moral degeneration of man.[1] This end is the time of the 'birth-pangs of the

[1] Cf. for instance the pictures, 4 Ezra v., 4-12 ; vi., 20-24.

Messiah' and culminates in the advent of the *Antichrist* who was originally a mythological figure, the Dragon in which chaos is personified, and is now interpreted as a pseudo-prophet or pseudo-Messiah or as a king like Antiochus IV, and later by the Christians as a Roman emperor.

The change occurs when God or his delegate, the Messiah or the 'Man' ('Son of Man'), appears, for now the figure of the Saviour is also mythologised. The figure of the Davidic king is replaced by the mythological figure of the 'Man' who will come in the clouds from heaven. Then will take place the resurrection of the dead and the last judgment. This is a forensic act, a judgment over the whole world, in face of which everyone must give account for his deeds.[1]

The cosmological and historical points of view are combined in the Jewish eschatology. The predominance of the cosmological is shown by the fact that the end is really the end of the world and its history. This end of history no longer belongs to history as such. Therefore it cannot be called the goal of history towards which the course of history moves by steps. The end is not the completion of history but its breaking-off, it is, so to speak, the death of the world due to its age.[2] The old world will be replaced by a new creation, and there is no continuity between the two Aeons. The very memory of the past will disappear and, with that, history vanishes. In the new Aeon vanity is passed away and times and years will be annihilated, and months and days and hours will be no more.[3]

In the Israelite conception of history, a goal for history

[1] Cf. 4 Ezra vii., 32-38.
[2] Cf. 4 Ezra v., 55 ; Syr. Baruch, lxxxv., 10 ; 4 Ezra iv., 48-50.
[3] Cf. 4 Ezra vii., 31 ; Slav. Enoch, lxv., 7 s.

is promised, but the realisation of the promise is conditional on the obedience of the people. This idea remained in the rabbinic literature. The Rabbis thought that God would realise the promised salvation if the people would only strictly observe the sabbath twice. But in the apocalyptic view the end comes of necessity at the time determined by God.

According to the Old Testament hope, salvation comprises the welfare of the people. Therefore the responsibility of the individual coincides with the responsibility of the whole people. In the apocalyptic view the individual is responsible for himself only, because the end will bring welfare and judgment at the same time, and the individual's future will be decided according to his works. And this judgment is a judgment over the whole world. Certainly, the welfare to come is also the welfare of the community, but the community is the community of the elect, the saints, and therefore not a community of a people or nation, but a community of individuals. Admittedly we do not always find this idea fully and consistently expressed. Sometimes the old and the new hopes are combined, as for instance in the so-called Psalms of Solomon.

(3) *In the New Testament* both the Old Testament view of history and the apocalyptic view are preserved but in such a way that the apocalyptic view prevails.

Today it is commonly accepted that the reign of God which Jesus proclaimed is the eschatological reign. The only point in dispute is whether Jesus thought that the reign of God was immediately imminent, indeed already dawning in his exorcisms, or whether he thought that it was already present in his person — what today is called 'realised eschatology'. With this is connected the question of what he thought about his own person.

But it is not disputed that Jesus understood his time as the time of decision, and that he thought that men's attitude to himself and his message was decisive for them. The time has now arrived in which the old promises and hopes will be fulfilled :

Blessed are the eyes which see what you see !
For I tell you :
Many prophets and kings desired to see what you see, and did not see it,
And to hear what you hear and did not hear it. (Luke x. 23 f.)

This is no time to mourn and fast. It is a time of joy like that of a wedding (Mark ii. 18). Satan's reign is now collapsing (Luke x. 18), and so on.

Jesus speaks of the 'Man' ('Son of Man'), that is, not of a historical but of a heavenly Saviour who will sit in judgment. He does not refer to the history of the people as the sphere in which the justice of God appears in punishing and rewarding. According to him, the judgment is wholly concentrated in the last judgment before which everyone is responsible for his works. True, his preaching is addressed to the people, but in such a manner that it is individuals who are called to follow him. The present people as a whole is an adulterous and sinful generation (Mark viii. 38, cf. viii. 12 ; Matt. xii. 45). He holds out no prospect for the future of the people and gives no promises, like Isaiah and Deutero-Isaiah, about the splendid future of Israel and the restoration of the house of David.

The preaching of Jesus differs from the apocalypses in so far as he does not give any picture of the coming welfare, except to say that it is life (Mark ix. 43, 45 etc.), and that the dead shall be raised from death to this life (Mark xii. 18-27). Symbolically, salvation can be described as a great banquet (Matt. viii. 11). But the quality of life will no more be an earthly one, but like that of the angels in heaven (Mark xii. 25).

The early Christian community carried on the eschatological preaching of Jesus and enriched it by taking over some themes from the Jewish apocalyptic. For instance, a little Jewish apocalyptic tract (or pamphlet) seems to be woven into Mark xiii, undergoing revision in the process from a Christian standpoint. At the end of it it is stated : 'But in those days, after that tribulation, the sun will be darkened, and the moon will not give its light, and the stars will fall from heaven, and the powers in the heaven will be shaken. And then they will see the Son of Man coming in clouds with great power and glory. And then he will send out the angels, and gather his elect from the four winds, from the ends of the earth to the ends of heaven.' Then the dead will be awakened and the judgment will take place. The righteous will enter into life, and the wicked will be handed over to eternal tribulation.

This is also the doctrine of Paul : 'For the Lord himself will descend from heaven with a cry of command, with the archangel's call, and with the sound of the trumpet of God. And the dead in Christ will rise first ; then we, who are alive, who are left, shall be caught up together with them in the clouds to meet the Lord in the air ; and so we shall always be with the Lord' (1 Thess. iv. 16 f.). Lo ! I tell you a mystery. We shall not all sleep but we shall all be changed, in a moment, in the twinkling of an eye, at the last trumpet. For the trumpet will sound, and the dead will be raised imperishable, and we shall be changed. (1 Cor. xv. 51 f.) For we must all appear before the judgment seat of Christ, so that each one may receive good or evil, according to what he has done in the body. (2 Cor. v. 10.)

Likewise the author of the Acts of the Apostles makes Paul say on the Areopagus at the end of his speech : 'The times of ignorance God overlooked, but now he commands all men everywhere to repent, because he has fixed a day on which he will judge the world in righteousness by a man whom he has appointed, and of this he has given assurances to all men by raising him from the dead' (Acts xvii. 30 f.).

This message of the coming end of the world runs through most of the New Testament, and for a time the conviction is retained and maintained in the face of doubts, that the end is at hand in the immediate future. As Paul writes to the Romans : the night is far spent, the day is at hand (xiii. 12). Likewise the author of 1 Peter writes : 'The end of all things is at hand' (iv. 7), and the author of Revelation : 'The time is near' (i. 3 ; xxii. 10 ; cf. Heb. x. 25 ; James v. 8).

It is true that themes from the Old Testament view of history are combined with the apocalyptic eschatology. For the Christian community took over the Old Testament from the Jews and understood itself as the 'Israel of God' (Gal. vi. 16), as the 'chosen race', as 'God's own people' (1 Peter ii. 9), as the 'Twelve tribes in dispersion' (James i. 1). Abraham is held to be the father of believers (Rom. iv. 1-12 etc. ; James ii. 21 ; 1 Clem. xxxi. 2 ; Barn. xiii. 7, etc.). The Christian community understands itself as the goal and consummation of the history of salvation, and therefore looks back into the history of Israel which has now reached its goal. The speech of Stephen reviews the history of Israel from Abraham to Solomon, using the old traditional pattern of the conflict between the divine leading and the people's reluctance. The sermon of Paul in Pisidian Antioch also gives a survey of Israelite history, seen as the story of divine guidance from the elected Fathers until David, with whom the goal of history is connected in the sending of Jesus. This view of history also underlies the enumeration of Old Testament examples as models of faith (Heb. xi.). Unity with Israel's history is very clearly expressed in the idea of the 'New Covenant'. Jeremiah had promised the New Covenant for the time of the end, and it is now realised by the death of Christ as the sacrifice of expiation (1 Cor. xi. 25 ; 2 Cor. iii. 6 ff. ; Gal. iv. 24 ; Heb. viii. 8 ff., etc.).

But we must not be misled by such sayings into supposing that the early Christian community understood itself as a real phenomenon of history, or that the relation to the Israelite people was understood as real historical continuity. There is no genealogical connection between the new people of God and the old, or, so far as there is, it is in principle irrelevant. For Abraham is the father of all believers, Gentiles as well as Jews. The continuity is not a continuity growing out of history but is one created by God. He has called a new people as his own people, and for this new people all the promises of the Old Testament will be fulfilled, indeed, they were originally given precisely for this new people. The Old Testament was read in the first place not as a historical document but as a book of revelations, as a book of the promises now fulfilled. It is now possible for the first time to know the meaning of Israel's history and of the words of the Old Testament. For now for the first time the divine counsel which was hitherto concealed is unveiled. It does not consist in the divine guidance of Israel's history as the Deuteronomic historiography understood it, in the sense that the justice of God could be known from the changing events of history. The content of the divine counsel is the eschatological events which have begun to happen with the incarnation of Christ, with his crucifixion, resurrection, and glorification, and which continue to happen with the conversion of the Gentiles and the constitution of the Church as the body of Christ, and which will reach their end in the expected last things.

The New Covenant is not grounded on an event of the history of the people as was the Old Covenant. For the death of Christ on which it is founded is not a 'historical event' to which one may look back as one may to the story of Moses. *The new people of God* has no real history, for it is the community of the end-time, an eschatological phenomenon. How could it have a history now when the world-time is finished and the end is imminent ! The consciousness of being the eschatological community is at the same time the consciousness of being taken out of the still existing world. The world is the sphere of uncleanness and sin, it is a foreign country for the Christians whose commonwealth is in heaven (Phil. iii. 20). Therefore neither the Christian community nor the individuals within it have any responsibility for the present world and its orders, for the tasks of society and the state. On the contrary, the believers must keep themselves pure from the world, that they may be 'blameless and innocent, children of God without blemish in the midst of a crooked and perverse generation, among whom you shine as lights in the world' (Phil. ii. 15).

Therefore no social programme can be developed but only negative ethics of abstinence and sanctification. In this sense the Old Testament commands remain in force, along with additional commands of Stoic philosophy. Even the Christian command of love is negative in so far as it demands unselfishness but does not set

36

concrete goals of acting. Obviously the ideal of asceticism enters here and there into the Christian ethic quite early.

To sum up. All this means that in early Christianity history is swallowed up in eschatology. The early Christian community understands itself not as a historical but as an eschatological phenomenon. It is conscious that it belongs no longer to the present world but to the new Aeon which is at the door. The question then is how long this consciousness can remain vivid, how long the expectation of the imminent end of the world can remain unshaken.

Obviously the fact that the expected coming of Christ failed to take place gave rise to disappointment and doubt. Therefore the admonitions and warnings to be vigilant and not to grow weary increased. The struggle against doubt became important — the doubt which says : 'Where is the promise of his coming ? For ever since the fathers fell asleep, all things have continued as they were from the beginning of creation' (2 Peter iii. 4). The answer is that God reckons with other times than men, for 'with the Lord one day is as a thousand years and a thousand years as one day'. And, furthermore, we must consider the forbearance of God who does not wish 'that any should perish, but that all should reach repentance'. Elsewhere it is simply said that the counsel of God is hidden : 'of that day or that hour no one knows, not even the angels in heaven, nor the Son, but only the Father' (Mark xiii. 32). But such answers could not provide a solution of the problem for any length of time.

IV

THE PROBLEM OF ESCHATOLOGY (A)

The Historicising of Eschatology in St. Paul and St. John. The Neutralising of Eschatology through Sacramentalism and the Hope of Immortality.

(1) THE problem of Eschatology grew out of the fact that the expected end of the world failed to arrive, that the 'Son of Man' did not appear in the clouds of heaven, that history went on, and that the eschatological community could not fail to recognise that it had become a historical phenomenon and that the Christian faith had taken on the shape of a new religion. This is made clear by two facts : (a) the historiography of the author of Luke and the Acts of the Apostles (b) the importance which tradition gained in the Christian community.

(a) Whereas Mark and Matthew wrote their Gospels not as historians but as preachers and teachers, Luke, as a historian, undertakes in his Gospel to represent the life of Christ. He assures us in his preface that he endeavoured, as a scrupulous historian, to use trustworthy sources for his report. In his Gospel not only does he provide a better connection of events than he found in Mark, but he also establishes a chronological connection with world-history, for instance in dating the birth of Jesus and the appearance of John the Baptist. Then he adds to his Gospel a history of the earliest Christian community, the beginning of its mission, and the missionary voyages of Paul until his captivity in Rome. The earliest Christian community in its eschatological consciousness would not have been interested in such an account. I may simply mention the fact that Luke gives speeches of Peter and Paul at important points in the story after the pattern of ancient historians.[1]

(b) It is obvious that the tradition had to gain increasing importance the more the eyewitnesses of the life of Jesus and the first generation of Christians died out. An early symptom of this is the use of the words παραδιδόναι — παραλαμβάνειν (deliver — receive) in Paul, and even more clearly the designation of delivered Christian doctrine as παραθήκη (deposit) in the Pastorals. The Pastorals are especially interested in the trustworthiness of the leaders of the community, whose duty it is to uphold the tradition. Indeed, the growth and development of the ecclesiastical office has its ground especially in the need to guarantee the safety of the tradition. The most important part of the tradition is the *doctrine*, because the community is not constituted on a national or social basis but by the word which calls the individuals into the community. The doctrine says what the content of faith is. Therefore the tradition can be named 'the word delivered from the beginning' (Polyc. *ad Phil.* vii. 2), 'the faith once for all delivered to the saints' (Jude iii). It is also called 'the delivered holy commandment', but in this case the tradition of ethical commandments may be included, as they are compiled in *Didache* 1-5 ; *Barn.* 19. One may also add the tradition of liturgical forms and uses (*Did.* 7-15) which coincide partly with the doctrine in so far as they are concentrations of it. Even Paul refers to such matters of tradition, and the postpauline literature much more.

[1] Cf. Hans Conzelmann, *Die Mitte der Zeit. Studien zur Theologie des Lukas* (1954) ; Martin Dibelius, *Aufsätze zur Apostelgeschichte*[2] (1953).

(2) But now we must try to see what position the Church, in becoming a world-historical phenomenon, can take up with regard to eschatology in view of the failure of the parousia of Christ to take place. How is the Church to understand the relation between history and eschatology ? A new understanding of eschatology, which appears for the first time in Paul and is radically developed in John, is the first stage in the solution of the problem.

(a) *The Pauline understanding of history* is determined by eschatology. When Paul looks back into the history of Israel, he does not see it as the history of the nation with its alternations of divine grace and the people's obstinacy, of sin and punishment, of repentance and forgiveness. For him the history of Israel is a unity, a unity of sin. By Adam, sin came into the world, and it was brought to its full development by the law of Moses. But the history into which Paul looks back is the history not of Israel only, but of all mankind. Both Jews and Gentiles are sinners and handed over to the wrath of God, for all the world must stand guilty before God (Rom. iii. 19). Therefore, the end of history cannot be the natural result of historical development, but only its breaking off, accomplished by God. But *sub specie Dei* the end is nevertheless the goal of history because, according to Paul, it is the grace of God by which the end is brought about, and grace will become effective just where sin is become mighty (Rom. v. 15, esp. v. 20 f. ; cf. Gal. iii. 19-22). To this extent Paul recognises a meaning in history, but not a meaning which is immanent in history itself. This meaning cannot be seen when history is regarded in itself ; for it is not grounded in meaningful historical actions and events, nor can it be discovered by the researches of a philosophy of history. The meaning is given by God, according to whose will the history of sin has the paradoxical meaning of being the relevant preparation for his grace.

It is clear that this view of history does not originate in the Israelite history as it is reported in the Old Testament. It is rather the apocalyptic view of history in so far as, according to Paul, the history of the past is the history of the whole of humanity and, as such, a history of sin. The past is 'the old Aeon' which is ruled by the Devil and its God, and which will endure only a very short time till the day of the parousia of Christ and the resurrection of the dead, the Last Judgment and the final establishment of the reign of God.

The apocalyptic view of history, however, is altered by Paul in a decisive manner in that, according to him, the history of humanity under law and sin has a meaning. In other words : Paul has interpreted the apocalyptic view of history on the basis of his anthropology. The Pauline view of history is the expression of his view of man : man can receive his life only by the grace of God, but he can receive the divine grace only when he knows himself annihilated before God ; therefore the sin into which man is plunged is paradoxically the presupposition for the reception of grace.

Paul has interpreted history in terms of this view of man. The law which came in between Adam and Christ must carry sin to its culminating point in order that grace can become mighty (Rom. v. 20). That this view of history is derived from anthropology is indicated by the fact that Paul can present the course of history from Adam, by the way of the law, to Christ, in the form of an autobiographical 'I' (Rom. vii. 7-25a).

I need give only a hint of the problem in which Paul involves himself by this view of history, namely that a peculiar difficulty arises concerning fulfilment of the promises. With this problem he wrestles in Rom. ix-xi. For our context it is important to see that Paul has decisively modified the current eschatology as well as the apocalyptic view of history. Naturally he cannot regard the eschatological consummation as the completion of the history of the Jewish nation, not even in the extended form depicted in Deutero-Isaiah and some later Jewish visions of the eschatological hope, namely, that the welfare of Israel is at the same time also the welfare of all peoples. On the contrary, his conception of the eschatological time of bliss is also determined by his anthropology.

To be sure, he does not abandon the apocalyptic picture of the future, of the parousia of Christ, of the resurrection of the dead, of the Last Judgment, of glory for those who believe and are justified. But the real bliss is righteousness, and with it freedom. The reign of God, he says, is righteousness and peace and joy in the Holy Spirit (Rom. xiv. 17). And that means : the conception of bliss is thought of with regard to the individual : and this state of bliss is already present. The believer who has received baptism is 'in Christ'. Therefore it is true that 'If any one is in Christ, he is a new creature' (2 Cor. v. 17), and that 'The old has passed away ; behold, the new has come' (*ibid.*). The New Aeon is already reality, for 'When the fullness of the time was come, God sent forth his Son' (Gal. iv. 4). The time of bliss, promised by Isaiah, is present : 'Behold, now is the acceptable time ; behold, now is the day of salvation' (2 Cor. vi. 2). The Gift of the Spirit, which the Jews expected to come at the time of the end, is now bestowed upon believers ; therefore they are now already 'sons of God' and free men instead of servants (Gal. iv. 6 f.).

Certainly, the gift of the Spirit is also called ἀπαρχή (first-fruits ; Rom. viii. 23) and ἀρραβών (guarantee ; 2 Cor. i, 22 ; v. 5). And πίστις (faith) is something preliminary in so far as the way of the believer goes from faith to sight (2 Cor. v. 7), and the seeing through a glass darkly will be succeeded by the seeing face to face (1 Cor. xiii. 12). But (1) *this hope is conceived in terms of the individual.* Paul no longer looks into the history of peoples and the world nor into a new history. For history has reached its end, since Christ is the end of the law (Rom. x. 4). And (2) for the believer who is 'in Christ' *the decisive event has already happened.* Neither death nor life nor any hostile power shall be able to separate us from the love of God which is in Christ Jesus our Lord (Rom. viii. 35-9). Whether we live or die, we are the Lord's (Rom. xiv. 7-9). The believer is even now free and master over all destiny :

For all things are yours . . .
whether the world or life or death,
or the present or the future,
all are yours ;
and you are Christ's, and Christ is God's. (1 Cor. iii. 21-3.)

But although the history of the nation and the world had lost interest for Paul, he brings to light another phenomenon, the historicity of man, the true historical life of the human being, the history which every one experiences for himself and by which he gains his real essence.

This history of the human person comes into being in the encounters which man experiences, whether with other people or with events, and in the decisions he takes in them. In these decisions man becomes himself, whereas the life of animals does not evolve through decisions but remains in the pattern given by nature.

43

The single animal is only a specimen of its genus, where-as the single man is an individual, a person. Therefore the life of a man is always one which stands before him and acquires its character as forfeited or as real by his decisions. What a man chooses in his decisions is basic-ally not this or that, but is himself as the man he is to be and intends to be, or as one who has forfeited his real life. For Paul human life is a life before God ; the real life then is the life confirmed by God, the forfeited life is the life condemned by God.

Man is free in his decisions from a formal point of view. Each encounter brings him into a new situation, and each situation is, so to speak, a call, a claiming of him as a free man. The question is whether he is able to hear the call — the call to be himself in free decision. It belongs to the historicity of man that he gains his essence in his decisions. But this means that he comes into every new situation as the man he has become through his previous decisions. The question is whether his new decisions are determined by his former decisions. If he is to be really free in his decisions then he must also be free from his former decisions, in other words from himself as he has become in his past.

For Paul, who sees man *sub specie Dei*, the call of the situation is the call of God. And Paul is convinced that man is not able to be free from his past, indeed, that he does not wish to be free but prefers to remain as he is. That is the essence of sin. This fact is expressed in the Pauline fight against the law as the means of salvation. Paul has seen that Jewish piety, the obedience under the law, is in reality a way of escaping from the genuine call of God, from decision. The pious Jew does not know that man has continually to become the one he is to be ; he thinks — of course, implicitly — that he is already the one he is to become. For he has anticipated all decisions by his resolution to obey the law. The commandments of law take from him the decisions required by the situation he meets. If the Jew thinks that he can be justified by God in virtue of his works, then he makes the presupposition that it is not himself who is required by God, but that God requires only this or that work which he can perform while himself remaining the same as he always was. It is clear that Paul speaks about typical Jewish behaviour without considering that there may be exceptions or modifications. His picture of the Jew is, so to speak, the picture of himself as he was before his conversion.

Paul's thought becomes still clearer in his description of Christian existence. To exist as Christian means to live in freedom, a freedom into which the believer is brought by the divine grace which appeared in Christ. The one justified by faith is set free from his past, from his sin, from himself. And he is set free for a real historical life in free decisions. This is made clear by the fact that the demands of God are summed up in the commandment of love, that is, in a commandment which does not consist in formulated statements and therefore can be depicted only in a negative way, as for instance 1 Cor. xiii : 'Love is not jealous or boastful ; it is not arrogant or rude ; love does not insist on its own way' and so on. When Paul says : 'Love is patient and kind ; love bears all things', and so on, then it is evident that the concrete commandments of love grow out of definite situations, encounters with one's fellow-men, and that obedience is rendered in decisions here and now.

The believers who are freed from law are admonished : '. . . be transformed by the renewal of your mind that you may prove what is the will of God, what is good and acceptable and perfect' (Rom. xii. 2). Paul prays for the Philippians : 'that your love may abound more and more with knowledge and all discernment, so that you may approve what is excellent' (Phil. i. 9 f.). Also from Phil. iv. 11 f. it is evident that the Christian life is not regulated by fixed prescriptions. Paul says : 'I know how to be abased and I know how to abound ; in any and all circumstances I have learned the secret of facing plenty and hunger, abundance and want'. Or he says to the Corinthians : 'To the Jew I became as a Jew . . . to those under the law I became as one under the law . . . to those outside the law I became as one outside the law . . . to the weak I became weak . . . I have become all things to all men . . .' (1 Cor. ix. 20-2).

The same freedom in responsible decision is expressed in the statement : 'All things are lawful for me, but not all things are helpful. All things are lawful for me, but I will not be enslaved by anything' (1 Cor. vi. 12), and again in the discussion of whether it is allowable to eat meat offered to idols, 1 Cor. viii. 1-13 ; x. 23-31. And it can only be a matter of decision how to obey the demand : 'Do all to the glory of God' (1 Cor. x. 31).

The real historicity of the Christian life becomes apparent also from the fact that this life is a continuous being on the way, between the 'no longer' and the 'not yet'. Paul as apprehended of Christ follows after, if that he may apprehend (Phil. iii. 12-14). The Christian life, therefore, is not static but dynamic, it is a permanent overcoming of the 'flesh' in the power of the Spirit (Gal. v. 17 ; Rom. viii. 12 ff.). There is a dialectical relation between the indicative and the imperative. The imperative : 'Let not sin therefore reign in your mortal body' is motivated by the indicative : 'For sin will have no dominion over you, since you are not under law but under grace' (Rom. vi. 12, 14). Likewise : 'If we live by the Spirit, let us also walk by the Spirit' (Gal. v. 25).

I leave it undecided how far Paul makes explicit thoughts contained in the preaching of Jesus. At all events the Pauline conception of historicity and his un-folding of the dialectic of Christian existence contains the solution of the problem of history and eschatology as it was raised by the delay of the parousia of Christ.

(b) *The conception of the eschatological event as happening in the present is still more radically unfolded in John*, because he gives up the expectation of future cosmic events, an expectation which Paul still retains.[1] For John the resur-rection of the dead and the last judgment are present in the coming of Jesus. It is evident that he formulates this statement in opposition to the traditional apocalyptic eschatology when he explicitly says :

> And this is the judgment,
> that the light has come into the world,
> and men loved darkness rather than light . . . (iii. 19.)

He interprets the κρίσις (or the κρίμα) by playing on the twofold sense of this word ; he understands the κρίσις, which is the judgment, as the separation which happens in the hearing of the word of Jesus :

> For judgment I came into this world,
> that those who do not see may see,
> and that those who see may become blind. (ix. 39.)

The believer has already passed the judgment, and he who does not believe is already condemned (iii. 18). The believer is already resurrected from death :

---

[1] There are a few verses in the Fourth Gospel containing the tradi-tional apocalyptic eschatology, but they are later additions by the ecclesiastical redaction of the Gospel, for instance, v. 28 f. ; vi. 51b-58.

> Truly, truly, I say to you,
> he who hears my word and believes him who sent me,
> has eternal life ;
> he does not come into judgment,
> but has passed from death to life.
> Truly, truly I say to you,
> the hour is coming and now is,
> when the dead will hear the voice of the Son of God,
> and those who hear will live.   (v. 24 f.)

Especially clear is the thought of the author in the dialogue between Jesus and Martha. Jesus assures Martha who is mourning for the death of her brother : 'Your brother will rise again'. Martha understands this in the traditional sense : 'I know that he will rise again in the resurrection at the last day'. But Jesus corrects her :

I am the resurrection and the life ;
he who believes in me though he die, yet shall he live,
and whoever lives and believes in me, shall never die.   (xi. 23-6.)

As for Paul, so for John the life of the believer is not a static state but a dynamic movement in the dialectic of indicative and imperative. The believer must still become what he already is, and he is already what he shall become. He is in the freedom into which he is brought by his faith, and which shows itself in obedience. The sermon of the vine says : the condition on which the branch abides in the vine is that it bear fruit ; but at the same time the condition that the branch bear fruit is that it abide in the vine (xv. 2-4).

John has expressed the dialectic of Christian existence with regard to a question which is not yet faced by Paul, namely, the dialectic between the freedom from sin and the necessity of constant confession of sin, of constant forgiveness. On the one hand he says : 'No one born

48

of God (and this is the believer) commits sin', and on the other hand : 'If we say we have no sin, we deceive ourselves and the truth is not in us. If we confess our sins, he is faithful and just and will forgive our sins' (1 John iii. 9 ; i. 8 f.).

Of course John also looks forward to a future perfection of the present life, but not, as Paul does, in the sense of the apocalyptic eschatology with its expectation of a cosmic catastrophe. John looks rather to the future of the individual believer after the end of his earthly life. He gives a new interpretation of the parousia of Christ. According to him, Jesus promises to his disciples that he will come again and receive them to himself into one of the many heavenly mansions (xiv. 2 f.). He asks his father that his disciples after his exaltation may be with him in glory (xvii. 24).

(3) For both Paul and John the present time is a 'time-between'. For Paul : between the resurrection of Christ and His expected parousia at the end of the world. For John : between the glorification of Jesus through his crucifixion (which is at the same time his exaltation) and the end of the earthly life of the individual believer. But for both of them this 'between' has not only chronological, but also essential, meaning. It is the dialectical 'between' which characterises the Christian existence as between 'no longer' and 'not yet'.

The question is whether this meaning of the 'time-between' could be retained ; and that is at the same time the question whether the Pauline and Johannine understanding of the relation of history and eschatology could be retained. The answer is that it could not. It is true that this understanding did not completely vanish in the postpauline literature, but on the whole it did, and the 'time-between' came to have merely chronological meaning.

The forgiveness of sin in baptism was no longer understood in the Pauline sense that 'the old man' is delivered to death and thereby freed from his past and from the determining power of sin. It was now regarded only as forgiveness of the guilt incurred by sin before baptism ; after baptism the Christian has to avoid new sins. The 'between' is now the limited time in which the Christian must prove true by his virtuous conduct, by fulfilling the demands of God or of the Lord in face of the imminent judgment where all will be judged according to their works.

The believer stands under the imperative, but the imperative no longer stands in the dialectic relation to the indicative, where to stand under the imperative means at the same time to stand under grace. Obedience is no longer the self-evident fruit of the gift of salvation, of justification and freedom, but is action done with the intention of effecting future salvation. To be sure, one still speaks of the presence of the salvation brought about by Christ. But the understanding of salvation is curtailed. Fundamentally salvation becomes simply the fact that by the forgiveness of sin in baptism a new beginning, a new chance, is procured, and now man must fulfil the condition for justification in the future judgment by his good works. Therefore man is again left to his own powers, and a striving after perfection arises and with it on the one hand the ideal of sanctification, on the other hand a statutory moralism.[1]

---

[1] A symptom of this is that the Pauline antithesis ἔργα-πίστις (works-faith) vanishes more and more, that the concept of πίστις (faith) loses its full meaning, and that the concept of ἐλευθερία (freedom) seldom occurs.

How in these conditions is the relation between history and eschatology understood ? How did the developing Church endure and overcome its disappointment that the parousia of Christ failed to materialise ?

The first answer is that the disappointment did not take place suddenly, nor everywhere at the same time. The 'time-between' was never reckoned by fixed months or years, as it once was in the Jewish apocalyptic and often later in the history of the Church ; the parousia of Christ was never expected on a fixed day ; it was believed that God had fixed the day and that no man knew it. By this faith the disappointment and the doubts which awoke here and there could be stilled, and it is a fact that the Christians gradually became accustomed to waiting. Certainly, in times of oppression or persecution the expectation of the near end of the world and the hope of it flamed up passionately. But, on the other hand, the Pastoral Epistles show that the Christians gradually slid into a manner of life which was both Christian and civic at the same time, and various admonitions here and there to be patient, waiting, and vigilant indicate the same.

But eschatology was never abandoned, rather the expected end of the world was removed into an indefinite future. This happened without any great shock, not only because the Christians became accustomed to waiting but also in consequence of the developing sacramentalism. Two effects of sacramentalism were : (1) The interest of the believers was directed not so much to the universal eschatology, the destiny of the world, as rather to the salvation of the individual soul ; to it a blessed immortality is guaranteed by the sacrament ; (2) The powers of the beyond, which will make an end of this world, are already working in the present, namely, in the sacraments which are administered by the Church.

This development took place as the Christian community spread in the Hellenistic world and in so doing became a community of cultic worship. In the Hellenistic Christian communities the figure of the eschatological Messiah or 'Son of Man' was more and more replaced by the figure of the κύριος, the Lord, who is present in the cult of the worshipping community and demonstrates his presence in pneumatic phenomena which occur in the worship.

The controversial question whether the title κύριος, Lord, was already given to Christ in the earliest community or for the first time in the Hellenistic churches may be left undiscussed. In any case the title Messiah became a proper name in Hellenistic Christianity, the title Son of Man disappeared, and the title Lord took the chief place.

In the presence of the Lord, salvation is in a certain manner present. But this presence is no longer regarded as it was in Paul and John, as working in the eschatological existence of the believers. The relation of the present eschatological existence to its future is conceived not as a dialectical one, but as a real one, namely, as an anticipation of the future.

To worship belongs also preaching, the word of truth, the Gospel of salvation which has revealed the mystery of God, which has brought life and immortality, and which has given knowledge, wisdom, and understanding (Col. i. 25 f. ; iv. 3 ; Eph. iii. 3 ; vi. 19 ; 2 Tim. i. 10, etc.). Therefore in a certain way salvation is present in this word and in the knowledge with which it endows the believers. To this extent the Pauline and Johannine conception of the presence of salvation is retained. But even that was restricted by the fact that the Lord who is present in his word came to be understood more and more as teacher, as lawgiver, and as example.

Primarily, Christ is present in the sacraments which mediate the powers of the beyond. According to Col. i. 13 f., God 'has delivered us from the dominion of darkness and transferred us to the kingdom of his beloved Son, in whom we have redemption, the forgiveness of sins'. This is said with regard not to the word, but to baptism, and it is characteristic for the further development. It finds its clearest expression in Ignatius of Antioch. He calls the Lord's Supper 'medicine of immortality, antidote against death' (Ign. *Eph.* xx. 2). In the sacramental worship occurs the eschatological event ; Ignatius says : 'If you frequently come together (namely to the Lord's Supper) the powers of Satan are destroyed' (*Eph.* xiii. 1).

Now that the sacramental worship is ruled by the Church officials, the office gains sacramental character. It is handed down by a sacramental act, ordination, and the officials who administer the sacraments receive the character of priests in contrast to laymen. So the Church is changed from a community of the saved into an institution of salvation. The Spirit is no longer a freely working power, but is bound to an office, and the believers are supported and surrounded by the ecclesiastical order.

The problem of sins committed after baptism was also to be solved sacramentally. This problem became urgent in the face of gross sins. For it was never in doubt that the penitent could find forgiveness for smaller sins, when he asked for it or the worshipping Church asked for it on his behalf. But the gross sinner, especially

53

the apostate, has lost the grace of baptism. But gradually the Church claims to be empowered to give forgiveness even to gross sinners, if they repent. So arose the sacrament of penance, by which, so to speak, the sacrament of baptism can be renewed.

In the sacramental Church eschatology is not abandoned, but it is neutralised in so far as the powers of the beyond are already working in the present. The interest in eschatology diminishes. And for this there is the further peculiar reason that the cosmic drama, which was expected in the future, was thought of as having in a certain sense already happened. The influence of the gnostic mythology was effective here. The Gnostics believed that, although there is to be an end of the world, the decisive event has already happened in that the heavenly Saviour came into this world and then left it and so prepared a way to the heavenly world of light for his adherents. His descent and ascent are combat with and victory over the hostile cosmic powers, which have incarcerated the heavenly sparks of light in human souls and then obstruct their way back into the heavenly home.

John used this myth of the descent and ascent of the heavenly Saviour to describe the work of Jesus, but divested it of its cosmological significance. But this cosmological aspect reappears in the Epistles to the Colossians and Ephesians. Here the work of Christ is described as a work of cosmic reconciliation by which the cosmic disorder is restored to order, for Christ has overcome the cosmic powers which revolted. In these epistles this cosmic mythology is combined with the traditional Christian understanding of the work of Christ, with the mythology standing in the background. The authors of the Epistles do not use gnostic tradition generally, but particular songs or liturgical texts in which the work of Christ was described in this manner. Fragments of such songs or texts are also woven into 1 Peter, 1 Tim., and more especially the letters of Ignatius of Antioch.[1]

Whereas according to Paul the victory of Christ over the cosmic powers is yet to be awaited as the events of the coming last time (1 Cor. xv. 24-6), in the other view the victory is already gained. The centre has 'been shifted, even if the expectation that Christ will one day return as the judge over the living and the dead is not abandoned. This can be observed in the terminology. For the words ἐπιφάνεια (appearing) and παρουσία (coming), which originally denoted the future coming of Christ, can now also be used to denote his earthly coming in the past.

The Church can now be conceived as the result of the cosmic victory of Christ, and can therefore be evaluated as an eschatological phenomenon, as is done in the Epistles to the Colossians and Ephesians. Speculations then arose which thought of the Church as pre-existent and later realised in history.[2]

---

[1] Cf. Heinrich Schlier, *Religionsgeschichtliche Untersuchungen zu den Ignatiusbriefen* (1929), and : *Christus und die Kirche im Epheserbrief* (1930) ; Ernst Käsemann, 'Eine urchristliche Taufliturgie', in : *Festschrift Rudolf Bultmann zum 65. Geburtstag* (1949), pp. 133-148 ; Rud. Bultmann, 'Bekenntnis- und Liedfragmente im ersten Petrusbrief', in : *Coniectanea Neotestamentica XI in honorem Antonii Friderichsen* (1947), pp. 1-14.

[2] Eph. v. 32 ; 2 Clem. 14 ; Hermas, *Vis.* II, 4, 1.

V

THE PROBLEM OF ESCHATOLOGY (B)[1]

The Secularising of Eschatology in Idealism. The Secularising of Eschatology in Materialism. The Belief in Progress.

WE have now to speak about the secularising of eschatology in Idealism and Materialism and about the belief in progress. But first we must survey the preceding ages in which all this was prepared.

(1) The longer the parousia failed to come and the end of the world was removed to an indefinite distance, the longer the Church had a history in this world, the more an interest in history developed.

(*a*) *The interest of the Church in its own history* had a further special cause. The Church claims to be founded by the Apostles, and the bishops claimed to be the successors of the Apostles. This claim had to be justified and therefore catalogues of bishops stretching back to the Apostles had to be compiled. The Church's consciousness of being the Apostolical Church is expressed in the words with which *Eusebius of Caesarea* begins his Church-history : 'I have proposed to write about the successors of the Holy Apostles and about the years which have passed from the time of our Saviour till our present time, all important events which have happened in the history of the Church and especially what concerns all persons who were guides and leaders in the prominent communities and have preached the divine word by word of

[1] For this chapter I am especially indebted to R. G. Collingwood, *The Idea of History* (1949), and Karl Löwith, *Meaning in History* (1949).

mouth or by writings'. Then the description of the heresies and of the fate of the Jews is to demonstrate the independence and purity of the Church, and its superiority is to be proved by the description of the persecutions and martyrdoms. In his *Chronicle* Eusebius had already set Church-history in the frame of world-history. In this he had predecessors of whose works only fragments are preserved. Theophilus of Antioch must be regarded as the oldest (in the last third of the second century). He wrote about the beginnings of human history. In A.D. 221 Julius Africanus composed a *Chronicle of the World*, beginning with its creation. He dated the incarnation of Christ in the year 5500 and expected his return in A.D. 500 at the end of the whole world-year of 6000 years. Hippolytus of Rome (born about A.D. 160/70) composed a chronicle which began with the creation of the world and extended to A.D. 234. He reckoned that of the 6000 years from the beginning until the end of the world 5738 years have now passed, and therefore the last day should be expected in 262 years. All these chronicles use the material of the Biblical tradition. Julius Africanus also makes use of Greek time calculations. But the basis of all these chronologies is the apocalyptic scheme of Daniel. Only Eusebius abandoned this apocalyptic reckoning and begins his history with Abraham, because only from Abraham's time onward can a trustworthy chronology be given. Eusebius combines erudition with scientific method and works scrupulously according to the documents (the sources).

With this, world-history in a strict sense comes into being for the first time. To the ancient historians for whom Greece or Rome was the point of orientation it was still unknown. It is symptomatic that a chronology now arose which comprehended the whole of history, whereas the Greeks dated events according to the Olympiads and the Romans according to the Consuls. For the new Christian chronology the birth of Christ is the centre of history from which time is reckoned backwards and forwards. The whole history of the world is divided into two parts and within those it is structured in epochs. Of course the scheme of the apocalyptic reckoning operates in this, but is now taken over in a scientific interest. Moreover, a basic divergence from the apocalyptic view is that the two halves of history are no longer distinguished as the Aeon of evil, ruled by the Satan, and the Aeon of salvation. This distinction was of course impossible, because the history of Israel recorded in the Old Testament belonged to the first half and also because the second half is not removed from earthly conditions, but is a time mixed with wrong, a time in which the Church has to suffer under political hostility and persecutions and through heresies.

The time before Christ was now understood as a time of preparation for the appearing of Christ and the Church, a time standing under divine providence. God sent his Son at a moment when the time was prepared by the Old Testament religion as well as by Greek philosophy. And a precondition for the coming of Christ and the propagation of the Gospel was the empire of Augustus with its 'Pax Romana'.

The whole course of history has now a meaning. Of course the conception of a divine plan in history originated in the Old Testament, in the apocalyptic writings, and in the theology of Paul. But there is now a decisive difference. In the Old Testament every event has a meaning because it signifies divine blessing or chastisement, and the whole process of history has its meaning as the education of the people. But one cannot speak of the course of history as an organic unity. That holds also for the apocalyptic view, for although apocalyptic regards the historical process as a unity it does not see it as a unity of historical development. Certainly, even for the Christian historians we cannot speak of a meaning which is immanent in the process of history. The meaning is imposed on history by the divine providence. But, in fact, the historians now believe that they can know the meaning of the historical actions and events within the historical process which is understood as an organic unity. And they are convinced that scientific historical study can detect the meaning in every case. A teleological view of history appears, and it only requires the secularising of the concept of providence for the meaning in history to be thought of as immanent.

This teleological view of history is something new and with it is connected a new understanding of time. Time and history were understood by the Ancients by analogy with the process of nature. The historical process runs in the eternal circle of time like the natural process in which the same phenomena ever return. It is with this view that Augustine principally comes into dispute on the ground of belief in creation. According to him, time and history are not an eternal cyclical movement ; time has a beginning, for it is created by God, and it has an end which God sets to it.

The Christian understanding of man is the decisive reason for this view. Augustine has taken it over from Paul, and he unfolds it mainly in opposition to the ancient manner of thinking. For ancient thought, man is an organic member of the cosmos, whereas for Augustine man has to be distinguished in principle from the world. The human soul, the human Ego, is now dis-

covered in a sense unknown to the Ancients. Erich
Frank has pointed out in a brilliant essay that Augustine's
understanding of the soul finds its expression in the shape
of monologue which replaces the older dialogue.[1] For
this the beginning of the 'Soliloquia' is characteristic.
Reason asks the Soul : 'What do you wish to understand ?' 'I wish to understand God and the Soul.'
'Nothing else ?' 'No, nothing else.' With Augustine
genuine autobiography comes into being.[2] His 'Confessions' are basically a monologue, a confession before
God. Man as a being distinct from the world aims at
the future and strives after something ultimate. He is
an individuality, a free person. *The problem of free will*,
unknown to the Ancients, now appears for the first time
in philosophical discussion. In his own will man has the
possibility of opposing himself to the good will of God.
He is free in his decisions for good and evil, and therewith
he has his own history. 'Thereby, every deed, every act
of volition or feeling acquired an importance which had
been unthought of before.'[3]

The conception of history which now appears is
determined by this understanding of man. First there
occur in history events which are new and decisive.
Of course, the ultimately decisive event is the appearance
of Christ. Nothing is comparable with it, but after it
the question at issue in history is the acceptance or the
refusal of Christian faith. Secondly, just as the life of
the individual goes onwards through decisions, so also
does the process of history. History begins with the

[1] Erich Frank, *Saint Augustine and Greek Thought* (1942). Cf. also
Erich Dinkler, 'Augustin's Geschichtsauffassung', in : *Schweizer Monats-
hefte* 34 (1954), pp. 514-26. Cf. also his book, *Die Anthropologie
Augustins* (1934).
[2] Cf. Georg Misch, *Geschichte der Autobiographie*, I[3] (1949/50).
Cf. Erich Frank, *l.c.* p.9.

fall of Adam who claimed to be independent of God. And since the time of Cain, who killed his brother and who founded the earthly empires, history is *the struggle between the 'Civitas terrena' and the 'Civitas Dei'*, between unbelief and faith. The struggle will not end until the consummation.[1] To be sure, Augustine does not think of this struggle as a historical development moving with historical necessity to the goal of the victory of the 'Civitas Dei'. He does not think of the 'Civitas Dei' as a factor of world-history, as identical with the visible constitutional Church, but as an invisible transcendent entity, an entity of the beyond to which man belongs by rebirth. The struggle between the 'Civitas terrena' and the 'Civitas Dei', therefore, is enacted in the history of individuals. For them history is the field of the testing of their obedience. But nevertheless, because the history of the 'Civitas Dei' is enacted invisibly within world-history, history gains a meaning as the field of decision.

The teleological view of history could be *secularised*, as could also Augustine's conception of the struggle between the 'Civitas terrena' and the 'Civitas Dei'. The concept of teleology made it possible to understand the struggle in secular terms as the struggle between the dark powers of nature and unreasonableness on the one hand, and the enlightened reason on the other. Even the idea of the fall of Adam as the origin of history could be taken over, if the fall was no longer understood as a unique historical event, but interpreted as a symbol of the fall of men from the good. The idea of the eschatological consummation could be interpreted as the victory of reason regarded as the necessary end of the historical development.

[1] Cf. Erich Dinkler, *l.c.* p. 519 ss.

(b) *Medieval historiography* did not as yet realise these possibilities. In its technical method it imitated the model of the Hellenistic and Roman historians ; in its conception of history it retained the outlook of the universalistic world-history and believed that the meaning of history could be known by detecting the divine plan within it. This meaning, however, is thought of not as immanent in history but as imposed on it by the transcendent divine counsel which uses human volitions and actions as its instruments. Therefore the history of the world is at the same time the history of salvation.

Medieval historiography also retains the conception of the eschatological goal of history, and in consequence of this it divides the historical process into epochs. Joachim of Fiore (1131–1202) divides it into three epochs according to the Father, the Son, and the Holy Ghost. The knowledge of the historian, therefore, comprehends not only the past but also the future. According to Joachim of Fiore the last epoch, that of the Holy Ghost, will begin in the year 1260 and will last until the return of Christ.

The medieval view of history also contains the possibility of secularisation — a secularisation which can take place after an epoch of critical historical research interested only in establishing historical facts, when the question about meaning in history awakes anew and with it an interest in interpreting the facts. Collingwood says : 'Nowadays, when we are less obsessed by the demand for critical accuracy and more interested in interpreting facts, we can look at it (*sc.* the medieval historiography) with a more friendly eye. We have so far gone back to the medieval view of history that we think of nations and civilisations as rising and falling in obedience to a law that has little to do with the purposes of the human beings that compose them, and we are perhaps not altogether ill-disposed to theories which teach that large-scale historical changes are due to some kind of dialectic working objectively and shaping the historical process by a necessity that does not depend on the human will.'[1] But this is an anticipation, and we must return to our context.

(c) *The historiography of the Renaissance* furthers the process of secularisation only indirectly, in so far as it adopts a profane understanding of history after the example of the Ancients. According to this it is man, not God, who sets the historical process going. The apocalyptic tradition with its scheme of the four world-empires of Daniel is abandoned and the idea of the eschatological end of history is dropped. In general, criticism of the legendary tradition is a main interest of the historians of the Renaissance, but no new under-standing of the essence of history arose.

(d) In 1681 appeared the famous 'Discours sur l'histoire universelle' of *J. B. Bossuet*, once more a world-history, standing in the tradition of teleological historiography. Bossuet strives to defend against the 'free-thinkers' the thesis that the divine wisdom rules the world in spite of the disorder which the human eye may perceive in history. For faith, the seeming disorder shows itself as an order in which all events are directed by the divine providence to carry history onwards to its end. This seems to be no more than the traditional view, but it must be recorded in our context because Bossuet especi-ally stresses the fact that the actions of men have to serve the divine plan without their knowing of it. He says :

Therefore it is that all who govern find themselves subject to a greater power. They do more or less than they intend,

[1] *l.c.* p. 56.

and their counsels have never failed to have unforeseen effects. Neither are they masters of the dispositions which past ages have given affairs, nor can they foresee what course futurity will take ; far less are they able to force it. . . . In a word, there is no human power that does not minister, whether it will or not, to other designs than its own. God only knows how to bring everything about to His will : and therefore everything is surprising to consider only particular causes ; and yet everything goes on with a regular progression.[1]

It is astonishing how akin this view of history is to the modern view, and it is easily comprehensible that Bossuet's conception could be secularised in the Hegelian notion of the 'Cunning of Reason' ('List der Vernunft').

(2) (a) In 1725 and 1730 appeared the 'Scienza nuova' (New Science) of Giovanni Battista Vico. In this work the theological teleology of history is transformed in a decisive manner. In our context we have to deal with it only from this point of view. In a later context it has to be considered in another aspect.

Vico, who was a loyal Catholic, was also convinced that history is guided by divine providence. But ultimately he neutralises the conception of providence as a transcendent power, for he understands the historical process as a development which is natural as well as providential. He calls his new 'science' a rational theology of divine providence and he is convinced that providence works as *lumen naturale* (natural light) or *sensus communis* (common sense). The course of history has its own inner necessity, given to it by God ; therefore God need not interfere with it. It is precisely in the historical decisions and free actions of men that history obeys this inner necessity. Here too appears the thought secularised by Hegel with his conception of the

[1] I cite the translation of K. Löwith, *l.c.* p. 142.

'Cunning of Reason'. The world 'has issued from a mind "often diverse, at times quite contrary and always superior" to the particular ends that men have proposed to themselves'. 'In history men do not know what they will, for something different from their selfish will is willed with them.'[1]

The idea of eschatology, of a goal and consummation of history, is eliminated by Vico's understanding of the historical development. For, according to him, the course of history is a cyclical one, running in the rhythm of *corso* and *ricorso* (course and recurrence) ; but about this we have to speak later. Here it is to be stressed that the cyclical course of history is, according to Vico, distinguished from the old idea of the return of all things[2] by the fact that the cycles follow each other in spiral progression. Although the stages of each cycle are parallel to each other, the cycles are by no means identical. The Christian barbarism out of which the Middle Ages grew is different from the ancient barbarism and so on. Therefore the historian cannot predict the future, for new events are always occurring in spite of the cyclical movement. But there never occurs a final, definitive happening, an eschatological perfection. If there is a salvation, then it is only within history in so far as a new cycle follows after the decay of an old one.

(b) The eighteenth century, to the beginning of which Vico belongs, is the century of *Enlightenment*. Here we cannot deal with its forerunners in the seventeenth century such as Locke and Berkeley, nor need we speak of Hume and the French philosophers of Enlightenment, nor Rousseau either. In our context our interest is directed only to the secularising of the theological teleology of history.

[1] K. Löwith, *l.c.* pp. 126, 127.   [2] Cf. above, pp. 23-24.

The general character of Enlightenment is the secularising of the whole of human life and thinking. The idea of teleology, however, remains and with it the question about meaning in history. The course of history is understood as progress from the dark era of the Middle Ages to enlightened thinking or, what means the same thing, from religion as superstition to science. In this view real history begins for the first time with scientific thinking and therefore the interest in history is not directed upon the pre-scientific time, and scientific thinking is not understood as growing out of the earlier time, but appears, so to speak, as a miracle. The idea of real historical development is therefore not conceived — or only in so far as the era of science is at the same time the era of erudition and civilisation. In this respect there is a progress which is to lead to a Utopian state of perfection, the state of universal enlightenment under the rule of reason. To this extent the idea of eschatological perfection is retained in a secularised form.

In this context we need not deal with the opposition to the Enlightenment on the part of Rousseau and Herder. But a few words must be said about the view of history of *Kant*, who derives from the Enlightenment, because in his critical philosophy the truths of the Christian faith and its view of history are secularised by being interpreted as philosophical truths. Kant preserves the idea of world-history as a teleological process. For, according to him, history is to be understood in the same way as nature as an unfolding according to a plan. The goal of this process is the realisation of the human being as rational and moral. This realisation will come about not only for the individual but also for mankind. History is necessary as the education of mankind for freedom, for all mankind will become free, rational, and moral. History, therefore, is the progress to rationality, to rational religion, to moral faith. 'Kant interprets the whole history of Christianity as a gradual advance from a religion of revelation to a religion of reason by which the Kingdom of God is realised as an ethical state on earth.' [1] The goal is the Kingdom of God not as a state of welfare outside history but as an ethical community on earth.

But Kant also preserved in a secularised form the Christian idea that history originated in the fall of Adam, and that it consists in the struggle between Good and Evil. According to him, it is Evil which brings the historical process into movement. The conversion of man to Christian faith is the inversion of his motives. For this to happen he requires divine power, because otherwise he would be thrown into fear and despair in face of the majesty of the moral law. It must be said that Kant's view of history is a moralistic secularising of the Christian teleology of history and its eschatology.

I need not deal with the continuation and modification of Kant's view of history by Fichte and Schelling. For their readiness to understand the historical process as a logical and necessary process or as the self-realisation of the Absolute is perfectly developed by *Hegel*. The secularising of Christian faith is carried out by him consciously and consistently. The history of salvation is projected on to the level of world-history. Hegel thinks that in this way the truth of Christian faith can definitively be validated. Philosophy has to bring to the purity of pure thinking what religion expresses in the form of images. Hegel preserves the Christian idea of the unity of world-history but he abandons the idea of providence as inadequate for philosophical thinking.

[1] According to K. Löwith, *l.c.* p. 244, n. 8.

The divine plan which gives history its unity must be understood as the 'absolute Mind' ('Geist'). This 'absolute Mind' realises itself in history according to the law of dialectic, namely, through the opposition of thesis and antithesis striving to unification in synthesis.

The historical process ruled by reason is a development which unfolds with logical necessity without removing human freedom and human passions. For it is precisely the 'Cunning of Reason' ('List der Vernunft') that free human actions which are subjectively motivated not by reason but by passion have to serve the universal development. Whereas according to Christian thinking men often do not know the real goal of their actions because it is God who guides history, this happens according to Hegel because in all actions it is reason which prevails. The goal of history is not an eschatological future but is the historical process itself by which the absolute Mind comes to itself in philosophical thinking. In a certain sense it may be said that the eschatological consummation is realised by the Christian religion. For, according to Hegel, the absolute Mind is not something static outside history but is itself within the historical development. Therefore Hegel can not only distinguish historical epochs, but he can concede to the Christian religion, of course in its secularised form, that it is the absolute religion. The Christian epoch is the decisive epoch in which man, free from all external authority, has gained his own relation to the absolute Mind. With Christ the time is fulfilled.

(3) The Hegelian dialectic of history was altered into dialectical materialism by *Karl Marx*. He was convinced that he had brought the philosophy of Hegel to its perfection. In fact, he took over from Hegel the idea of the historical process as a dialectical movement which

runs with logical necessity through the opposites of thesis and antithesis. But the moving power according to him is not Mind but Matter in the sense of the powers which are immanent in economic life. All historical phenomena originate in economic-social conditions. The social structure corresponds to the conditions of production. Political systems, art, religion, and philosophy are nothing but ideological superstructure. The movement of history stems from the opposition of economic classes, it proceeds as the struggle between these opposing groups and therefore through crises and catastrophes according to the law of necessity. The 'Cunning of Reason' is to intensify the opposition and thereby lead to catastrophe. Every ruling society already contains the forces which are to overcome it, or it develops them. This is true of the present capitalistic society within which the opposition between bourgeoisie and proletariat has become so great that a revolution must come. The very development of capitalism itself has dissolved the ties of the old tradition and invalidated all patriarchal and human relationships. The proletariat is the carrier of the future. Its dictatorship will lead from an epoch of necessity into the realm of freedom, into the Kingdom of God without God. Then all oppositions of classes, all differences between oppressors and oppressed will vanish. The 'Communist Manifesto' of 1848 is a messianic message — as has been well said, a secularised eschatology.

The Christian teleology of history and its eschatology are completely secularised in the outlook of historical materialism. It may even be said that the Christian view of history as the struggle between Good and Evil is secularised in so far as the economic opposition between oppressors and oppressed, between exploiters and exploited, brings about the historical movement. Exploitation is the original sin.

(4) Another kind of secularising of the Christian teleology of history with which we now have to deal is the belief in progress. Certainly, belief in progress has one root in Idealism and Materialism. But the shape in which it came to reign in the nineteenth century does not derive from Hegel or Marx, but from the Enlightenment of the eighteenth century.

According to Hegel progress is the course of history, moving with logical necessity, and it has its meaning in the increasing rule of reason. According to Marx progress is the result of crisis and revolutions, and has a concrete goal in an ideal economic state. The faith in progress which in the nineteenth century became a universal world-view, replacing the Christian faith in large measure, is the faith in progress without limits. This progress takes place as though of itself through the development of science and technics and by the progressive mastery over nature rendered possible by them. Its meaning is the bringing about of ever-increasing welfare.

This belief in progress is not in accord with the Christian faith, indeed, it is opposed to it. It originated in the polemics against the Christian belief in providence. Voltaire, who intended to sketch a philosophy of history as a deliverance from the Christian teleology of history, begins with an argument against Bossuet.[1] Then he disputes in opposition to Leibniz the possibility of a theodicy. It is, according to him, impossible to justify God in the face of events, as, for instance, the earthquake of Lisbon (1755) proves. But there is, of course, a progress in history, namely, the progress of knowledge ;

[1] Cf. above, p. 63–64.

and the meaning in history is the fact that men become richer in knowledge and thereby in welfare. Voltaire expected only a moderate rate of progress, and did not foster enthusiastic hopes. Yet he saw the eighteenth century as an almost ideal state ; only the fight against the Church and Christian superstition had now to be taken up. To this belongs the criticism of the Bible. The traditional chronology, based partly upon Biblical statements, is shaken by the discovery of China and its literature, as are also the traditional division of world-history into epochs and the idea of the unity of world-history.

Turgot, disciple of Voltaire, is also an advocate of a purely secular faith in progress. He concedes to Christianity the merit of inspiring the movement of progress. But he too replaces the divine providence by the natural law of progress. In him there is already something like the Hegelian 'Cunning of Reason' to be found, for he is convinced that unreasonableness and human passions have also to serve progress. His optimistic faith in progress leads him to the opinion that commerce and politics will 'reunite finally all the parts of the globe and the whole mass of humankind'. Progress, 'alternating between calm and agitation, good and bad, marches constantly, though slowly, toward greater perfection'.[1]

Condorcet also believes in the unlimited perfectibility of man and in progress which is accelerated by the perfection of knowledge and will lead to the welfare of humanity.[2] Truth, freedom, and equality are synonyms, according to him, and a victory of truth is at the same time a step to political freedom and equality. Certainly,

[1] The translation of Löwith, *l.c.* p. 100.

[2] About Condorcet, cf. Wilhelm Alff, 'Einige Themen der Aufklärung nach den Schriften Condorcets', in : *Aufklärung*, II (1953), pp. 242-55.

the way goes through revolutions, and the goal can be realised only step by step by education. The stage of progress already reached allows a prediction of the future in which even the natural constitution of man will be perfected to such a degree that death itself will be postponed. Historiography also belongs to the knowledge which must be developed, and it has to be an exact science by analogy with natural science. Historiography transformed into sociology allows for human foresight and replaces divine providence.

Auguste Comte was a disciple of Condorcet. He called his philosophy *philosophie positive*, because he wished to distinguish it from every theological and metaphysical theory. It should be based only upon positive facts. According to him, the task of historiography as well as of natural science is to establish pure facts and to know their causal connection by laws discovered by induction. In this way historiography is to be transformed into sociology. According to him, the idea of evolution is validated by history because it teaches us to understand nature, as Darwin has shown. So the positive philosophy of Comte points to a continuous teleological evolution of humanity, whose law plays the rôle of providence. *La marche fondamentale du développement humain* goes in three steps : (1) The stage of childhood is the stage of theology ; it is the Christian epoch ; (2) The stage of youth is the stage of metaphysics or abstract thinking ; (3) The stage of manhood is the stage of science or positive philosophy, beginning with Bacon, Galileo, and Descartes. In this context Comte ascribes a special importance not to the Christian religion, but to the Catholic Church so long as it was striving for independence of political powers through its organisation. For order is necessary for progress. By means of the positive philosophy mankind will take a fundamental step towards welfare, and a splendid picture of the future is painted : the end of militarism and wars, the rule of industrialism led by science. A universal religion of humanity will reign. The task is *réorganiser, sans Dieu ni roi, par le culte systématique de l'humanité.*

In a similar way *Proudhon* replaces the Christian religion by human atheism as the last step of mental and moral freedom. He also believes in natural progress and fights against belief in providence. According to him, what is called providence is nothing but the collective instinct, the universal reason. However, he abstains from enthusiastic predictions. For the way will go through crisis, and the present is, according to him, a time of dissolution.

To sum up. We have travelled a long way through the centuries, and we have seen how the Christian view of history became secularised. The main points are the following :

(1) The idea of the unity of history is retained at least in general.

(2) Likewise the idea of the teleological course of history is retained, but the concept of providence is replaced by the idea of progress promoted by science.

(3) The idea of eschatological perfection is transformed into that of the ever-increasing welfare of humanity.

But this optimistic faith in progress is threatened, and the facts which are to destroy it are already at the door.

VI

HISTORICISM AND THE NATURALISATION OF HISTORY

(The Abandonment of the Question of the Meaning in History)

Scepticism and Relativism. Vico and Herder. Romanticism. Oswald Spengler and Arnold J. Toynbee.

(1) (*a*) THE philosophers of the Enlightment believed in the unlimited perfectibility of man and in the power of man, or at least of enlightened man, to determine the course of history. And even if the historical process leads to results which were neither foreseen nor intended, the 'Cunning of Reason' was thought of as working for progress. Man, enlightened by science, knows the way into the future which leads to the ever greater welfare of humanity. For such optimism history has indeed a meaning. And with regard to this optimism even Marx agrees with the Enlightenment and with Hegel in that he also believes that the course of history is directed by reason.

Hegel, however, had been conscious that history, seen apart from faith in reason, 'forms a picture of most fearful aspect and excites the profoundest emotions and the most hopeless sadness'[1], for passions and wickedness are ruling powers in world-history. He does not believe primarily in the goodness and perfectibility of man,

---

[1] Cf. K. Löwith, *l.c.* p. 53.

but in reason which rules history in spite of human unreasonableness.

But how is it when history is seen without this faith in reason ? The faith in human goodness and perfectibility — can it remain steadfast ? The optimism of the Enlightenment — can it remain unshaken ? The earthquake of Lisbon, for instance, was a frightening event. And in the first lecture we have seen that the French Revolution had results contrary to its intention : military dictatorship instead of a liberal constitution, imperialism instead of a federation of free nations, war instead of peace.[1] And the actual course of the nineteenth century — did it justify the faith of the Enlightenment ?

Certainly the belief in progress remained vivid during the nineteenth century and seemed to be validated by the development of science and technics. But voices of scepticism grew loud, especially that of *Jacob Burckhardt*.[2] He denied the possibility of philosophy of history in general. He contested Hegel's doctrine of reason and what he called Hegel's bold anticipation of a plan of the world. Certainly, all happenings have also a mental side and mind is imperishable, but mind is subject to change and that not in a rectilinear direction. The essence of history is change ; there is only one constant substance : 'Our starting-point is the only remaining and for us possible centre, the suffering, striving and acting man, as he is and was and ever shall be'.

In saying this Burckhardt abandoned the idea of a uniform world-history. History shows not only changes but also variety and differences which cannot be seen as united by a reasonable principle. There are only repeti-

[1] See above, p. 3.
[2] The following quotations are taken from his lectures, 'Weltgeschichtliche Betrachtungen'.

tions, constant trends, typical phenomena, because man is always and everywhere the same. Certainly, there is the true and the good, but what at any given time is true and good is subject to conditions of time. 'In individual cases it does not matter by which colours the conceptions of good and evil are modified . . ., but the question is only whether man follows them dutifully as they are, sacrificing his selfishness, or not.' 'The sacrificing of one's life for others certainly already happened amongst the lake-dwellers.' 'If already in old times man gave his life for others, then we have not advanced any further from that time.' It is an illusion to speak of 'moral progress', as Buckle did. 'Mind was already complete in the earliest times.' Burckhardt turns with sarcasm against the opinion of the Enlightenment that man is essentially good and needs only enlightenment for his goodness to become sovereign. 'The secret reservation in this is that today it is easier and safer to gain money. When that is threatened then the high feeling in question will collapse.' History begins with the awakening consciousness of man, with the breaking with nature. 'But at the same time there still remains enough for man to be characterised as a ravening beast.'

Burckhardt attacks the optimistic faith in progress on the point of good and bad fortune in history. The judgments whether this or that event was a piece of good fortune, or whether this or that epoch was a happy one, are completely subjective. 'It is our deep and ridiculous selfishness which esteems as happy such times as have something similar to our own nature, and which esteems as praiseworthy the past times and actions upon which our actual present life and our relative well-being are grounded. Just as if the world and world-history were only existent for our sake.' The phrase 'good fortune' should be eliminated from world-history, only the phrase 'bad fortune' has its right, for evil rules in history, and though it is indispensable as a power moving history, nevertheless it always leads into bad fortune. 'It makes a frightening picture to imagine the sum of despair and distress which is presupposed, for instance, by the building of the old world-monarchies.' There seems to be no other consolation than the fact that bad fortune can have happy consequences. But we should be economical with this consolation because we do not have a standard of judgment for these losses of good fortune. Burckhardt arrives at the resigned judgment: 'good and bad may have balanced each other in general in the different periods and cultures. But in regard to history we should abandon the question about good and bad fortune. Ripeness is all. Instead of happiness the goal of clever men, *nolentium* or *volentium*, will be knowledge.'

In France, the most enlightened country, many intellectuals became conscious of the senselessness of material progress, and there grew up a nihilism which found its expression in the writings of Flaubert and Baudelaire, as Karl Löwith has described.[1] 'The world is drawing to a close', that is the judgment of Baudelaire. The criticism of Western civilisation and the faith in progress by Kierkegaard and Nietzsche, Dostoiewski and Tolstoi is differentiated in its aims, but they are all uniformly critical. And today after two world wars? I think the judgment of Erich Frank is right: 'It is the strange irony of our time that all progress in science and civilisation, nay, in moral and social consciousness, is turned eventually into a means for war and destruction. Even those peoples who do their utmost to prevent such a tragic reversal are forced to submit to the necessity of

[1] K. Löwith, *Meaning in History*, pp. 96-8.

history. To the extent to which man, through his reason, has learned to control nature, he has fallen victim to the catastrophes of history. Thus his dream that he may be entirely free to shape his future according to the ideals of his own reason is frustrated by history. Man is thwarted by man himself, by his own nature.' 'For such a point of view even the idea of humanity appears only as one "ideology" among many, as the expression of a definite historical and social situation.'[1]

(b) The historiography of the nineteenth century was not disturbed either by Burckhardt or by Nietzsche. Whether influenced by Hegel or not, whether it reflected about its method or not — on the whole it arrived at some form of *relativism*. It acknowledged change as historical law and denied the absolute value of judgments and knowledge, and it confirmed the dependence of all thinking and valuing on their time and culture. Later on we have to speak about the influence of Romanticism. Now it is sufficient to emphasise the fact that historiography was interested in knowing the casual connection of the events, and that a relativism developed, whether any particular historian was conscious of that or not. This is the epoch of the so-called *historicism* which in fact understands history by analogy with nature. Historiography seems to have the task of establishing the facts and of finding out the laws of their connection. It has taken over the idea of evolution, though only with regard to single epochs and spheres of culture, not with regard to history as a whole. It tries to eliminate the subjectivity of the historian and to avoid every value-judgment. Historiography is purely a science of facts, but it does not raise the question of what a historical fact is.[2]

[1] Er. Frank, Philos. Underst. and Relig. Truth, pp. 121, 122.
[2] Cf. Collingwood, *l.c.* p. 132.

This historicism, plus the despair about detecting any meaning in history and the consequent abandoning of belief in progress are the presuppositions of the book by Oswald Spengler *Der Untergang des Abendlandes* (*The Decline of the West*). Here historicism is, so to speak, completely swallowed up by naturalism. But the origin of this consistent reduction of history to nature lies far back. To some extent it revives the ancient understanding of the historical process as a cyclical movement.

(2*a*) This idea was taken up and developed in the eighteenth century by *Giambattista Vico* (1668–1744). We have already seen how in his view of history the idea of the divine providence was neutralised, and how he eliminated the idea of the eschatological consummation of history.[1] In our context we have to consider how he understood *the historical process as moving in cycles*. Each cycle passes in three stages. The beginning is the primitive age of gods, the age of barbarism. It is followed by the heroic age of aristocratic constitutions, represented for Greece by the Homeric period, for Europe by the Middle Ages. Then follows the classical age in which thinking rules over imagination, prose over poetry, and so on. In this age the free republics and monarchies grew up inspired by the belief in the equality of all mankind. The cycle ends with exhaustion and decay, with relapse into barbarism, and from this a new cycle begins as *ricorso* (recurrence).

This is, so to speak, a natural history of humanity. Indeed, Vico calls the object of his 'New Science' the common nature of peoples. Nature is not to be understood as a transcendent power always working in the same way. It is always growing ; *natura nascendo* is his formula. Vico has historicised the concept of nature,

[1] Cf. above, p. 65.

but at the same time it must be said that he has naturalised the conception of history. His presupposition is that the same disposition for certain forms of life and development is common to all men and peoples, the *sensus communis* (common sense). In the course of history differences develop in consequence of the different natural conditions, but the essential marks are always the same in each age.[1]

(*b*) The work of Vico proved ineffectual for a long time, till today in fact. But his view of history had a parallel in the work of Johann Gottfried Herder, *Ideen zur Philosophie der Geschichte der Menschheit* (1784–91).[2] We need not decide whether he knew Vico and was influenced by him. Herder also reduced human history to natural history. He understood nature and history from the concept of evolution and begins his history of humanity with the description of the cosmic and geological evolution, ending with the life of animals, the highest species of which is humanity. Humanity, therefore, is the summit of natural evolution. Herder reflects, for instance, about the relationship between monkeys and men, and he explains the difference between animal and man completely by means of physiological anthropology. The first decisive difference is the erect walking of man. He says : 'With regard to man all is ordered according to his present figure. Out of this, everything in history can be explained, nothing without it. On the erect figure depends the formation of the brain and finally of humanity. Man in distinction from lower nature builds a mental (spiritual) world, developing step by step to

[1] Concerning Vico, cf. besides the relevant chapters in Collingwood and Löwith ; Erich Auerbach, 'Giambattista Vico und die Idee der Philosophie' in : *Homentage a Antoni Rubio Lluch* (1936).

[2] Concerning Herder, cf. besides the chapter in Collingwood ; H. G. Gadamer, *Volk und Geschichte im Denken Herders* (1942).

humanity.' Herder traces back the establishment of the mental (spiritual) world to the development of the soul according to laws of psychology.

Herder can characterise humanity as a preparation, as a bud for a future flower, namely, transcendent existence in immortality. Therefore one may think that he distinguishes between nature and mind, and, indeed, his thoughts are not completely clear. But in any case it is clear that he understands human history in a completely naturalistic manner. The laws of cultural evolution are laws of nature, and he can say : 'The whole of human history is a natural history of human powers, actions, impulses according to space and time'. However, he conceives the laws of nature not in the same way as mathematical physics does, but as a play of living forces working in history. Humanity is also a result of these forces. For humanity is 'reason and fairness' or 'mind, fairness, kindness and human feeling', and these march onward with natural necessity, because they are the conditions for the continuity of human order and prove to be the persistent element in history. Herder, therefore, does not deal with the belief in the moral progress of humanity by means of virtue.

Herder does not know Vico's idea of the cycles. Rather he divides human history into different types or races. Human nature is not uniform but differentiated into types. These types do not originate in different historical experiences but in nature which distributes types of peculiar and unchangeable character. The character is originally formed by the conditions of life and by the earliest actions and occupations. What is effective in each people is the 'mind of the people' ('Volksgeist') which expresses itself especially in poetry. Each people follows its own way to achieve humanity.

'The whole history of peoples appears . . . as a school of competitive running to obtain the fair crown of humanity and the dignity of man.'

It is evident that the concept of evolution toward humanity is in conflict with that of natural evolution, for humanity is uniform. Indeed, Herder is not always quite clear.

Perhaps we may say that eschatology is working in a secularised manner in Herder's idea of the realm of human organisation as a system of mental (spiritual) powers. But that would be in contradiction to his conviction that each historical age and each people as well as each age of the individual has the centre of its blissfulness in itself and that it is not allowed to judge earlier times and peoples according to a measure of other times and to understand history as progress toward perfection, as did the Enlightenment. The earliest age of humanity is not to be judged as barbarism, but it 'breathes the healthy mind of childhood'. Herder also values the German Middle Ages, without failing to recognise its dark side, the quarrels of the nations. He says : 'The constitution of the German communities was in world-history the shell, so to speak, within which the remaining culture was safeguarded from the storm of life and the common mind of Europe developed and became slowly and secretly ripe for working upon all the countries of our earth'. And though he criticised the medieval Catholic Church, he finished with the judgment : 'I fully appreciate the value which many hierarchical institutions still have for us ; I see the need within which they were constructed, and I am sojourning in the solemn twilight of their venerable institutions and buildings. It is invaluable as the rude envelope of tradition which could endure the storm of the barbarians, and it bears witness to power as well as to reflection.' He adds, however : 'But it could scarcely have constant value for all times. When the fruit becomes ripe, the shell breaks.'

History is a play of the natural powers with which nature has endowed man. The investigation of history does not detect any meaning which might give unity to the whole and the course of the centuries does not lead to a perfection — if one will not take humanity as perfection. Herder contests the concept of progress held by the Enlightenment, and he says : 'Philosopher, seeing only the fundamental base of your abstractions, do you see the world ?· the harmony of the whole ?' Indeed, to see the harmony of the whole may be called the fundamental motif of Herder's view of history, and it can hardly be denied that this view of history is essentially an aesthetic one.

(3) The influence of Herder upon *Romanticism* was an extraordinary one, of course, alongside the influence of such men as Rousseau and Hamann. In Romanticism there was a real taste for history as part of its contest against the Enlightenment. The past was no longer negatively judged as a dark time lacking in enlightened reasonable knowledge, but positively as a time to which one thought oneself akin because the same irrational powers are to be observed within it as one feels working in oneself. These powers are working in all cultural fields and reach their greatest efficacy in the creative power of the I, the person, above all in religion and poetry. Romanticism was especially interested in the poetry of the past, in popular songs and popular fairy-tales and in medieval art (from which interest the per-fection of the cathedral of Cologne originated, but also the romantic admiration of ruined castles and the regret-table building of churches in imitation of the Gothic

style). With the predilection for the Middle Ages was not seldom connected an inclination toward the Catholic Church, as it is expressed in the paper of Novalis 'Die Christenheit oder Europa' (1799). There were also many conversions.

Herder's notion that culture is not to be judged according to an objective measure of reason, and that every place and every time has its own meaning and law led to *historical relativism*.[1] One result of this was a new conception of law, from which the so-called historical school of law grew up. According to this school, law is constituted not by objective rules but by history. There is no natural right but only positive (*i.e.* concrete historical) right. There are no ethical rules which all mankind is obliged to obey, but each time has its own ethics. The interest is directed not to the objective but to the subjective, to 'Erlebnis' (experience). In poetry the important thing is the 'Erlebnis', not the poetical work. 'Erlebnis' means becoming conscious of the irrational powers of life. This is at bottom an aesthetic view, directed to history as well as to nature ; and, in fact, historical events are understood as natural events.

The historiography of the nineteenth century is deeply influenced by Romanticism. Certainly, it has freed itself from the cult of 'Erlebnis' and from aestheticism, but it understands the historical process by analogy with nature.[2]

(4a) The understanding of history became radically naturalistic in Oswald Spengler's book *Der Untergang des Abendlandes* (*The Decline of the West*), as I have already mentioned.[3] The sub-title of this book is 'Outlines of a Morphology of World-History'. This is a hint of

[1] See above, p. 78.   [2] Cf. above, pp. 78.
[3] See above, p. 79.

his naturalistic view, as is his characterisation of cultures (or civilisations) as 'Lebewesen (living beings, animals) of the highest grade'. I do not know to what extent Spengler is indebted to Vico or to Herder. In any case he also holds that history is not a unity, and that its course is not progress. Rather the whole of history falls into cycles, that is, into a sequence of single civilisations which are closed in themselves and have their own character. There is no continuity in history. The civilisations are like the monads of Leibniz, as Colling-wood rightly says. There is only sequence in time, one succeeds the other. The seclusion of the single civilisations is so consistently conceived by Spengler that, for example, science, mathematics, and philosophy in each civilisation are something peculiar to it, and there is no unity between the mental lives of the different civilisations. In each of them the same process is repeated from the rise of the primitive barbarism of archaic times to the classical age in which political organisation, law, and science are developing and finally to the decay into the barbarism of civilisation. Each cycle has its time. Therefore it is possible to make a diagnosis of the present and to perceive in which stage our civilisation is placed and, in accordance with that, to predict the future. Spengler himself says that he undertakes for the first time to define history in advance.

Civilisations are like plants which grow up, flourish, become ripe, and wither. As it is impossible to raise the question about meaning in the life of nature, so with regard to history. Of course, it goes without saying that there is no eschatological perfection. Spengler expressly denies that there is a historical course within which the present takes over the mental tradition of the past and develops it further.

I will only briefly mention that for the sake of his theory Spengler makes violent constructions. He has detected an 'Arabic civilisation' which includes most of the first millennium after Christ, and thereby he breaks up antiquity by regarding its later epoch, Hellenism, as a completely new civilisation, and at the same time he breaks up Christianity into supposed different religions. I will also no more than mention that it is an inconsistency when he combines with his prophecy a challenge for decision, namely, the call to the Germans to erect a 'Prussian socialism' and thus to become rulers of the future. In our context only the methodical principles interest us.

(b) It seems that *Arnold J. Toynbee* is to be grouped with Oswald Spengler in so far as he too stands in the line which leads from Vico over Herder to Spengler. For him, too, history is not a unity ; its course is not a progress leading to perfection, and one may not, therefore, raise the question about its meaning. And he, too, divides history into the histories of single groups, of societies. His interest is directed towards the societies which left the primitive stage behind and developed civilisation. These were the first to experience history. He enumerates twenty-six civilisations of which sixteen have passed away ; their histories are finished. Five great civilisations are still living ; Western Christianity, Eastern Christianity, Islam, Hinduism, and the Far-Eastern civilisation. He endeavours to detect the law of history by comparative research (*vergleichende Erforschung*) into the civilisations. He asks : how have we to explain the origin, the growth, and the decay of the civilisations ?

Certainly, it may be said, as Collingwood does, that Toynbee follows the method of natural science by establishing facts, connecting them, and establishing laws of evolution. His conception of civilisations also corresponds to the way of thinking of natural science. For Toynbee has only a formal concept of civilisation, like, for instance, the concept of maturity, and not a material concept, like, for instance, Herder's concept of humanity. Each society has its own civilisation, and so far as this is unique it is not possible to speak of the unity of mind and to understand history as the history of mind. Toynbee seems not to be conscious that the historian himself stands within history, and that an investigation of history teaches : *tua res agitur*. On the contrary, he stands over against history as a disinterested spectator, like the scientist who has no share in the natural events he observes.

Nevertheless, it seems to me that Collingwood goes too far in saying : 'his general conception of history is ultimately naturalistic'. That would be appropriate to Spengler. But Toynbee differs from Spengler in many respects. First, in that, according to him, the different societies are not shut off from one another. Many civilisations are connected by affiliations, and therefore tradition is handed down in the course of history. Above all, the historical course of the various societies is not determined simply by natural factors. Toynbee himself warns us not 'to apply to historical thought, which is a study of living creatures, a scientific method, derived from the study of inanimate nature'. He argues against historians who reduce historical events to the natural factors of race or geographical surroundings. The movement of history is brought about by an unpredictable factor, namely, the behaviour of a nation in a critical situation.

Toynbee has detected the law of Challenge and Response. Every society is brought both at the beginning and in the course of its history into situations which are challenges to it and provide an ordeal for the challenged. The decisive question is the answer given to the challenge. On it depends whether the society enters into history or continues its history. The challenge is a stimulus, for example the necessity for a people in unfavourable geographical conditions to procure a home on new ground, or fatal blows such as hostile assaults or oppression by a foreign power, or internal or domestic troubles such as slavery, or problems growing out of the development of technics. Everything depends on whether a response is made to the challenge, and this cannot be calculated in advance. To this extent the necessity of natural development is modified ; a certain measure of freedom and responsibility is ascribed to men. But the law of challenge and response assumes the aspect of a natural law again, when Toynbee tries to decide when a challenge would be an excessive one and when a less severe one, which is the optimum in regard to which the answer is determined, and when he introduces the notion of the *élan vital* in explaining the growth of a society which has entered into history.

But finally it must be said that according to Toynbee religions are not simply expressions of civilisation as they are in Spengler, but have an exceptional position, especially Christianity.[1] Christianity grew out of the decay of the Hellenistic society, and perhaps it will not only survive the decay of the Western civilisation, but even increase 'in wisdom and stature as the result of a fresh experience of secular catastrophe'. Certainly, although it is not the task of a religion 'to serve for the cyclical process of rebirth', it may nevertheless retain its meaning in such a process. In this sense Christianity

[1] For this, cf. especially A. J. Toynbee, *Civilisation on Trial* (1948).

may be called the ever new and greatest event of human history. Perhaps some day it will conquer all other high religions and become the world-religion as the heir of all other religions.

Something like secularised eschatology may resound in these thoughts, and one may ask how it is to be reconciled with Toynbee's basic view of history. Toynbee himself strives for reconciliation when he says : 'If religion is a chariot, it looks as if the wheels on which it mounts toward heaven may be the periodic downfalls of civilisation on earth. It looks as if the movement of civilisation may be cyclic and recurrent, while the movement of religion may be on a single continuous upward line. The continuous upward movement of religion may be served and promoted by the cyclical movement of civilisations round the cycle of birth-death-birth.

But Toynbee reflects also upon the possibility that a third kind of society may arise after the two which have existed up till now, the primitive and the civilised, the time of which is limited. The future society would embrace the whole world, and it would be 'embodied in a single world-wide and enduring representative in the shape of the Christian Church'. But he distinguishes this kind of hope from the old eschatology by expressly denying that the Kingdom of God could in this way be realised on earth. For it to be otherwise, the nature of man would have to be altered so that the will for evil vanished. But as long as original sin exists in mankind, there will never be a society which does not need institutions grounded in power. Therefore the 'victorious Church Militant on Earth' will only be a province of the Kingdom of God, but a province in which the citizens of the heavenly commonwealth have to live and breathe and labour in an element that is not their native element'.

In this context Toynbee denies Frazer's statement that the Christian religion and civilisation are opposites, and that the Christian religion, because it is individualistic, destroys culture, which is grounded in a social ethos. For the question arises why civilisation should be interested in religious progress. Toynbee answers : 'Religious progress means spiritual progress, and spirit means personality. Therefore religious progress must take place in the spiritual life of personalities.' The thesis of Frazer is wrong 'because I think it is based on a fundamental misconception of what the nature of souls or personalities is'.

But now a new question arises. Should not history be understood as the history of the spiritual life of personalities ? What is the real subject of history ? Humanity ? The nations ? Civilisation ? The societies ? — Or man ? With this we have reached the theme of the next chapter.

VII

THE QUESTION OF MAN IN HISTORY

The Conception of Man in Greece and in the Bible. Individualism in the West. Realism in the West.

WE ended the last lecture with the question : is not man the real subject of history ? Now we have to consider how man has been understood in the course of our Western history, in order to find an answer to this question. Therefore we have to return again to the origins of our Western history in the Biblical tradition and in Greek culture. Let us begin with the Greek understanding of man.

(1) With regard to the question of how man understood himself in Greece we have to distinguish between the citizen of the Polis (the City-State) in the Classical age and the conception of man found in Greek science and philosophy.[1] Both agree, however, in essential trends : (a) in the peculiar Greek individualism, according to which man is an autonomous person who is conscious of his *freedom* ; (b) in the thought that the individual is a member of an *order*. That may seem to be a contradiction, but in fact is not, because the order was conceived as one into which the individual fits organically, since the law of the order agrees with the law of

---

[1] Cf. Max Pohlenz, *Der hellenische Mensch* (1947) ; Richard Harder, *Eigenart der Griechen* (1949) ; Günther Bornkamm, *Mensch und Gott in der griechischen Antike* (1950). Cf. also Rud. Bultmann, *Das Urchristentum im Rahmen der antiken Religionen* [2] (1954). English translation, *Primitive Christianity in its Contemporary Setting* (1956).

his own nature. The very nature of man is believed to be mind or reason, and reason is also the origin of the order both of the Polis and of the Cosmos.

Freedom within the Polis is not arbitrary freedom. It is bound by the law (Nomos) in which it is grounded. This freedom contains within it right and duty. It endows the individual with the honour of responsibility for the whole. For the authority of the Nomos does not stem from a tradition given in history, but from the idea of law conceived by reason. The development of this idea was to be of the greatest importance for the history of the West.

I can no more than mention how the peculiar dialectic of freedom and order expresses itself within the different fields of life in Greece, the rôle which it plays in the contests (Agon), athletic games, as well as in discussions and philosophical dialogues. Nor can I here give an account of the fate which this dialectic experienced in Greek history, and how its breakdown was one reason for the collapse of Greek democracy.

The dialectic between freedom and order appears also in Greek science and philosophy. The question about truth was answered not by the authority of a tradition but by methodical thinking. In thinking, the individual is independently guided by his reason, and he acknowledges as truth only that of which he is convinced by reason. But at the same time science established community because reason is a common gift of all mankind and truth is to be found in free discussion.

A main theme of philosophical discussion is the relation between individual and Cosmos. The attempt to understand the Cosmos originated in the question about its Arché, its origin, out of which its unity and its lawful order grow. Rational thinking detects the unity and the lawful order ; in other words, it perceives the world to be a Cosmos, a harmonious whole, the structure of which can be explained by mathematics. Reason or mind is the origin of the cosmic order as well as the very nature of man. Therefore man can be understood as a member of the Cosmos, not a stranger within the world, but secured within the Cosmos as his home.[1]

Precisely stated, the Cosmos is the whole within which the material stuff becomes moulded into harmonious unity by the power of organising reason, and all coming to be and passing away is ruled by the eternal laws of reason.[2] Man is understood in the same way in so far as he has to master his sensuality, the physical impulses of his body, by his rational mind. Because his genuine nature is mind or reason, ethics are not conceived as commandments of an authority, but from the view-point of rational education and culture by which the genuine nature of man is to be realised.

Education is the task of learning.[3] It goes without saying that everyone is striving for good, but only reason can say what the good is. Likewise it goes without saying that the man who knows the good will realise it by his actions, that the will will follow reason. According to the dialectic between freedom and law, between autonomy and limiting measure, the goal of education is the culture of the individual. This, however, does not mean that his personal peculiarity is to be cultivated in an individualistic sense. The individual

[1] In this context I cannot deal with pessimistic voices in Greek literature. On this theme see, for instance, William Chase Green, *Moira* (1948) ; André-Jean Festugière, *Personal Religion among the Greeks* (1954).

[2] I cannot, of course, here describe the discussion and the differences, modifications or variations, through which this understanding took shape.

[3] Cf. Werner Jaeger, *Paideia* [3] (1947).

has to realise *the ideal image of man*, an image which, like a work of art, represents a harmonious figure in which body and soul have found their right proportion. A sign of this is the ethical terminology, *e.g.* κόσμιος (harmonious), εὐσχήμων (well-shaped), and so on. Therefore ὕβρις (exceeding all measure) is the real evil, and σωφροσύνη (self-control) and δικαιοσύνη (Justice) are the chief virtues.

In all this the freedom of man is presupposed. The question about the freedom of the will did not arise in philosophical research in ancient Greece, because it was believed that the will follows reason, and reason has its own law which cannot be altered by any fate. Later on the question about freedom of will was raised by Stoic philosophers. But the problem was only the relation of free decision to the causal determination of events and not, as later in Augustine, the question about the essence and power of the will as such. Therefore the Stoic philosophers did not deny freedom of decision.[1]

In consequence of all this — namely, the conception of the nature of man as mind, as reason — the historicity of man was not detected by Greek thinking, nor was history perceived as a peculiar theme of philosophy, as has been shown in the second lecture. According to Greek thinking man cannot really be touched by encounters, but encounters can only be for him occasion and material for unfolding and shaping his timeless nature. In principle the future cannot bring anything new in so far as man is independent of time in realising his real nature. This thought was consistently developed by the Stoic philosophers. Their ideal of the wise man is the man who is independent of all that can encounter

[1] For the theme of freedom, cf. Max Pohlenz, *Griechische Freiheit* (1955).

him, good as well as evil, because he is untouchable in his interior, in his mind. He lives completely unhistorically, enclosing himself against everything that the future may bring.

With this the Greek conception of the relation between man and God agrees. The transcendence of God is thought of as his timelessness, for his essence is mind. He is transcendent over against everything concrete and particular which comes to be and passes away within time. But his transcendence is not conceived in terms of the independence and absolute freedom of his will, nor of his being a God who might ever come into this world. Man has to venerate God with awe (εὐσέβεια) and to take care that he does not offend him by violating the measure, by hubris ; but by acts of hubris man would also insult his own nature. Inasmuch as he is mind, he is related to God and shares, so to speak, in the transcendence of mind over against the material, sensual, and historical world. Man is free over against God in so far as it is just his obligation to the divine order which makes him free ; for the law of this order is also the law of his own nature. Violation of this order revenges itself, but it cannot destroy human nature ; it does not involve man in debt to God, which needs divine forgiveness ; it is not a positive wrong but is error which man can overcome by education. Man is not qualified by his past, he does not convey his past into his present. In other words, he has not become aware of his historicity.

(2) In depicting *the Biblical conception of man* I will point to the difference between Old Testament and New Testament only incidentally, because their conception of man is the same in its main trends.

In the Bible man is seen in his relatedness to God.

First of all therefore we must elucidate the difference between the Biblical and the Greek conception of God. In the Bible the transcendence of God is conceived not as the transcendence of mind over against the material and sensual world, as timelessness over against the course of history, but as absolute authority. God is absolutely independent of every other power, he is the ever-coming, ever-encountering God. He is, of course, the eternal God, but he is a God who acts, and acts in history. He is the almighty creator of the world, and is not conceived as the law of mind which forms the Cosmos into a harmonious shape which can be recognised by reason. Certainly, the pious Israelite admires and praises the wisdom of God, but he does not see it in the rational cosmic structure. Therefore the conceptions of providence and theodicy, discussed by the Stoic philosophers, are strange to Biblical thinking. If the question about the nature of God should be raised, the answer has to be that the nature of God is will. All that man sees and experiences has its ground in the will of God.

Therefore God is the God of history and therewith always someone new, always the God who comes to men in historical encounters. He is the God who guides history to an end which for later Jewish and Christian thinking is the eschatological goal.[1] The concept of man is in accord with this. Certainly, man consists of body (or flesh) and soul. But soul is not the rational mind which is related to the divine mind. There is no trace of the Greek conception of an ideal image of man which is to be formed according to the law of mind like a work of art, nor does the idea of rational education and culture exist. The very nature of man is his will, which can be good or evil. Its goodness consists in obedience to the

[1] See above, Chap. III.

demands of God ; its badness is disobedience and revolt against the will of God. The good or bad will of man manifests itself also in his attitude to God's guidance in history, either thankfully accepting the divine ordinances and praising God, or else resisting and grumbling.

The demands of God are not rules grounded in reason, but are given for the first time in the Old Testament by a tradition whose authority is grounded in history. And it is characteristic that in the Old Testament there is on the whole no distinction between cultic and moral commandments. In the preaching of the prophets and even more in the New Testament, however, the ethical commandments are recognised as the real demands of God, and the cultic and ritual commandments are eliminated.

The ethical demands, however, are not orientated towards an ideal human image of the individual but towards the concrete life of community. And the community is not thought of as constituted by rational law like the Greek Polis, but as given by the history of the people within which everyone is joined with his fellowmen. The main content of the ethical commandments in the Old Testament, therefore, is right and justice and love and mercy by which the relationship between neighbours is kept sound. In the New Testament, of course, the demand of love is paramount. The authority of the commandments is the authority of God who, in being will, wills community. He brings about and also demands community between men in and through history, and he puts himself into community with men.

The peculiar dialectic between freedom and law is unknown to the Bible. The conception of freedom is not known at all in the Old Testament, neither does it appear in the preaching of Jesus. It occurred for the first time in Paul. But although the word is taken over from Hellenistic language, it no longer has the sense of freedom belonging to man as a rational being, but has become, so to speak, a historical conception, for it means the freedom of man from his sin, from his past which weighs upon him, from himself. This freedom does not belong to the timeless nature of man, but can only happen as an event.

This event happens by the grace of God. For, since the nature of man is will, he is evil in his totality when his will is evil, and so inevitably enters each present moment as evil. Only the grace of God can make him free from evil. In the Old Testament this is not clearly recognised with all its consequences from the beginning. So long as cultic trespasses have the same value as moral, man is indeed dependent on the grace of God, but he receives it by the cultic offerings which are ordained by God for this very end. In the prophetic preaching the insight is gained that man does not become a new person by cultic offerings, and this preaching therefore demands renewal of heart, *i.e.* will, or hopes that God himself will produce such renewal. So also Jesus says that good and evil come out of the heart of man. He praises the pure in heart, and he demands that we love God with all our heart. The demands of the Sermon on the Mount are nothing but the demand for conversion and renewal of will ; for they teach that the will of God is not ful-filled by fulfilling the commandments of law ; on the contrary, God demands a good will. When man be-comes aware that he has disregarded the will of God and when he confesses before God his unworthiness, then he can be sure that God forgives him.

Jesus complains : 'How can you speak good when you are evil' (Matt. xii. 34). Paul developed the knowledge of the evil within man. According to him, man is not free but prisoner of his sin. He recognises that man fails to fulfil the will of God, not only by violating the commandments of law, but even in fulfilling them, because man imagines that he is able by fulfilling the law to make a claim on the grace of God. For this means trusting in his own power and failing to realise that man as a whole is a prisoner of sin and has to become an entirely new person. This can happen only by the grace of God, revealed in Christ. Man who opens himself to this grace is 'in Christ' and therefore a 'new creature'.

Paul makes clear the real essence of sin when he recognises boasting as the chief sin. Sin is the striving to stand before God in one's own strength, to secure one's life instead of to receive it — and therewith oneself — purely as a gift from God. Behind this striving lies man's fear of giving himself up, the desire to secure himself and therefore the clinging to that which is at his disposal, be it earthly goods or be it works performed according to the commandments of the law. Lastly it is fear in face of the future, fear in the face of God himself, for God is the ever-coming God. Already in the Old Testament this is the real sin : not to trust in what God has done in the past of his people and not to be open for what he will do in the future, not to expose oneself to the future but to endeavour to have disposal over it. Isaiah had already admonished the people against such behaviour :

In returning and rest you shall be saved ;
In quietness and in confidence shall be your strength. (xxx. 15.)

Paul hears the Lord speaking to him : 'My grace is sufficient for you, for my power is made perfect in weakness', and he confesses : 'I will all the more gladly boast of my weakness, that the power of Christ may rest upon me . . . for when I am weak, then I am strong' (2 Cor. xii. 9 f.). Faith is faith in God 'who gives life to the dead and calls into existence the things that do not exist' (Rom. iv. 17). Faith is therefore faith in the future which God bestows on man, in the coming God. And this means that in the Bible man is understood in his historicity, as qualified by his past and required by his future.

(3) The Greek conception of man came to life again in a new form in the idealist philosophy as a whole. I will only describe the typical trends of the idealist image of man in so far as in Germany at least it came into opposition to the Biblical concept, and, on the other hand, also influenced evangelical theology in a considerable measure until the days of the so-called dialectical theology.

In *Idealism* the very nature of man was understood, as it was in Greece, as mind. Mind or reason, however, was primarily understood as practical reason which, according to Kant, has the primacy over theoretical reason. Practical reason is independent of theoretical reason and has its own ground in conscience which knows itself challenged by the duty to be virtuous. In other words the nature of man is the moral will. This will is in tension with the impulses ('Triebe') of the physical body, with sensuality ('Sinnlichkeit'); duty stands over against inclination. The dualistic relation between mind and sensuality ('Geist and Sinnlichkeit') can be understood as in Greece : sensuality is the material which is to be ruled and formed by mind, that the pure figure of man may be shaped. The conception of education and culture gains the same importance as in Greece. And, as in Greece, the forming of character can be conceived by analogy with artistic production. Indeed there is more than analogy. According to Plato, the teaching of mathematics is the basis of education, and, according to Schiller, aesthetic culture is its principal method. In both cases the presupposition is that education according to the law of measure and order leads to the harmonious figure of man.

The idea of the dialectic relation between freedom and law, as characteristic for human beings, is also common to the Ancients and to Idealism. It is formulated by *Goethe* in the sentence : 'Only law can give us freedom'. *Schiller* characterises the 'most mature man of the time in the end of the (eighteenth) century' as 'free by reason, strong by laws'. In the poem *The Eleusinian Festival* he says about man : 'Only by his morals can he be free and mighty'. This dialectic is most clearly unfolded by *Kant*. He recognised that will, if it is to be really free, must be determined not by empirical motives but by a law, in obeying which man becomes free from natural (sensual) impulses. The law has to be a 'categorical imperative'. That means a law which is valid without condition, a law which is the expression of practical reason, a law to which man assents because it is the self-determination of the rational will.

Here there appears a characteristic difference from ancient thought which is brought about by modern empirical science, represented most of all by Newton. Modern natural science has divested nature of Gods, as Schiller complains in the poem *The Gods of Greece* :

> Like the dead striking of the pendulum-clock
> Nature, deprived of Gods,
> Slavishly serves the law of gravity.

Therefore the law corresponding to freedom is not the cosmic order recognised by theoretical reason, but the law of a supersensible world. It cannot be the object of theoretical reason but only of faith ; of a faith, however, which is grounded in necessity *a priori*, a faith which understands the moral law, experienced in conscience, as divine demand. With this the faith is also given that the sensual world, object of theoretical reason, belongs to a moral world-order. From this conviction arises the postulate of immortality.

In spite of all parallels with ancient thought the characteristic difference becomes clear. It is that according to Idealism the will is paramount in human essence. Schiller says :

> You must receive God (the Deity) in your will,
> then he descends from his Throne of the universe.
> The severe chain of the law binds only
> the slavish mind which repudiates it.
> With the reluctance of man
> so the majesty of God vanishes.

Therefore the relation between mind and sensuality is not only and not always understood by analogy with artistic production, but also as a struggle between two opposite principles. In this the influence of the Christian tradition is at work, as it appears in Kant. He transformed the Christian conception of original sin into the doctrine of 'radical evil'. According to him, within man there is an inclination to evil, which is not indeed explicable, but is a fact. Therefore the inversion of motives is demanded. Against the doctrine of radical evil, however, opposition arose, especially from Schiller. But Schiller, too, can describe the relation between mind and sensuality as one of opposites between which decision is demanded :

> Between pleasure of sensuality and peace of soul
> there is only the dangerous choice.

Schiller admonishes the men who are striving for a higher life of mind :

> Throw away the fear, threatening earthly being,
> you must flee from the limited gloomy life
> into the realm of the ideal.

And he says : 'The good and the right are always obliged to engage in combat. The enemy will never be overcome'.

Finally, a difference from the Ancients may be seen in the fact that the figure into which man is obliged to shape himself by his moral will is not so much the ideal image of man in general as rather the figure of individuality which is, however, an expression of humanity. Let me again cite a word of Schiller :

No-one be equal to the other, but everyone be equal to the Highest.
How is it to be done ? Everyone be perfected in himself.

Therefore it may be said : on the one hand, the Greek image of man is taken over by Idealism, but, on the other hand, it is modified by the influence of the Christian tradition. The will of man is now acknowledged as a decisive trait of human nature. With this the historicity of man begins to be recognised, although it is not yet clearly perceived. For the freedom of man is understood as the power over himself which is not called in question either by his past or by his future. Man is not seen as qualified by his past. The future is thought of as being at the disposal of man — not, of course, the future of fate, of events which occur, but the future of the human self, because man has the power by his will to remain as he is, or to become ever more himself within all events. Fate, therefore, is not experienced as the judging or blessing power, but as the Stoic philosophers also taught, as the occasion for proving man's own power. It is in this sense that Schiller, looking on the tragic figures of Shakespeare, speaks about the 'great gigantic fate which raises man in crushing man'.

Faith in the mental power of the individual leads Idealism to trust in the improvement and perfection of humanity. In this optimism Idealism is related to the Enlightenment, although it was interested only in moral evolution and its consequences for political order and not in material welfare. And it goes without saying that in Idealism optimism was grounded upon the evolution not of science and technics, but of moral education and the self-perfection of the individuals.

(4) It would now be proper to speak about the understanding of man in *Romanticism*. But I must restrict myself and I will only say that the understanding of man in Romanticism corresponds to its understanding of history.[1] The historical process is understood as ruled by irrational powers, and the individual is understood as an irrational mystery, unfolding itself according to its own peculiar law. Respect for originality, reverence for genius are characteristic of Romanticism, and they are symptoms of its aesthetic view of humanity.

But we must deal in greater detail with *Realism*; I do not mean with the philosophical school of Realism, but with a peculiar type of mental behaviour. Realism in this sense conceived as reality only what can be perceived by the senses and can be explained in its structure by rational thinking. Of course, perceiving senses and rational thinking themselves belong to this reality. Realism, therefore, does not accept the idealistic dualism between mind and nature, but holds that mind belongs

[1] See above, p. 83.

to nature, and understands man as a natural phenomenon. Just as nature is seen as ruled by the law of causality, so also the life of man and human community are understood as ruled by this law. Therefore sociology and economics are sciences which originate from the realistic understanding of man.

As *Erich Auerbach* has shown in his brilliant book *Mimesis*,[1] in the ancient literature the realistic view of human life is to be found only in literature of the lower or middle style, in comedy and satire, as distinct from high literature. Auerbach has also shown that it is through the influence of the Christian understanding of man that the realistic view of life enters into high literature. Now too for the first time the everyday life of man is seen as the field of serious problematic and tragic happenings. In consequence of this the historical and social forces at work in everyday life came into consciousness and became interesting. In our context I cannot sketch the history of Realism from its beginning in ancient literature through the Middle Ages and Renaissance till the present day, but must be content to give a survey of modern Realism in contrast to Idealism.

It can be said that the sceptic *Michel de Montaigne* (1533–92) inaugurated modern Realism by describing in his *Essays* 'La Condition humaine' (the human situation) his own life as representing any human life. Here for the first time the life of a human being, just as his own particular life, becomes problematic, and the consciousness of the insecurity of human existence begins to arise.

[1] Erich Auerbach, *Mimesis. Dargestellte Wirklichkeit in der abendländischen Literatur*, (first ed., 1946). See also the important Essay of Friedrich Gogarten 'Das abendländische Geschichtsdenken. Bemerkungen zu dem Buch von Erich Auerbach *Mimesis*' in *Zeitschr. f. Theologie u. Kirche*, 51 (1954), 270–360.

This Realism which takes human daily life seriously and sees its problematic and tragic nature found its expression in the literature of the eighteenth century especially in England and France. In English literature, however, the serious view is veiled at first by humour as, for instance, in Sterne, Fielding, and Smollett, and later in Dickens and Thackeray. But even in these novelists the problems of social life in the different classes are well recognised and brought into consciousness — problems which later are the subject of the novels of Galsworthy, Meredith, and others, and once again the subject of comedy in Wilde and Shaw.

For the development of serious Realism the French novel was of the greatest weight. In this the French Revolution was of special importance. For, as Auerbach stresses, it was the first of the great movements in modern times in which large masses took part. It resulted in the various convulsions which spread over the whole of Europe. The consequence for the understanding of man was this, 'that the social basis upon which man lives is not firm even for one moment but is incessantly changed by various convulsions'.[1] *Stendhal* can be regarded as the originator of this modern Realism by his description of man as imbedded in the whole of the political and social reality which is constantly in process of development. Beside him *Honoré de Balzac* must be named. He not only sets man in the frame of temporal and social conditions but tries to depict the atmosphere which rules in the *milieu*, the environment. For him 'every sphere of life becomes a moral and sensual atmosphere which gives a peculiar character to landscape, dwelling, furniture, tools, clothes, body, character, acquaintances, sentiments, actions and occurrences of man, and the general

[1] *l.c.* p. 404.

situation of the time appears as the embracing atmosphere of the whole'.[1] The title which Balzac gave to the corpus of his novels is 'Comédie humaine'.

The realistic view of human life and its problematic and tragic character was carried further by *Flaubert* and finally by *Émile Zola*. For him the social problem of the society of the present is the main theme. His interest went beyond the purely aesthetic, for, by his description of the problems, he intends to make clear the responsibility of man for his world.

I pass over German literature within which the realistic moral novel is represented by Fontane and the Swiss Jeremias Gotthelf. There was also Realism in dramatic poetry, especially in Gerhard Hauptmann. He and Jeremias Gotthelf also stressed the responsibility of man for his time.

It is a question whether the most recent novels are still to be characterised as realistic. At all events they show the consequences to which Realism leads as long as it only depicts the world in so far as it can be perceived with the senses and explained by rational research, the world within which all things have become problematic so that man cannot perceive fixed orders which can give a hold for his existence. Auerbach gives a picture of the most recent novels by characterising Virginia Woolf, Marcel Proust, and James Joyce. In the view of these authors there seems to be no objective reality distinct from the subjective consciousness of the persons. These authors, as Auerbach says, have discovered a method of reducing reality to a manifold and ambiguous reflection of consciousness.

The interest no longer lies in the history of the persons and in the entire course of their life. On the contrary,

[1] *l.c.* p. 419.

the author is convinced that in moments chosen at random the whole of the personal life is contained. The analysis of the occasional moment unveils something totally new and elementary, the fullness of reality and the depth of life contained in every moment. In this moment a deeper reality, so to speak a more real reality, appears, which is relatively independent of the disputed and wavering orders within which men are struggling and despairing. It lies below all this as our everyday life. It is difficult to describe this reality. It is not a metaphysical substance, but it is the ever-increasing result of the whole of our experiences and hopes, of all our aims in interpreting our life and our encounters, it forms itself apart from our purpose and consciousness, but it comes into consciousness in moments of reflection.

In contrast to Idealism, Realism has recognised the historicity of man, and that with increasing clearness. The older Realism, as represented by Flaubert and Zola or by the social drama of G. Hauptmann, understood man in his historicity in the sense that it recognised man as being at the mercy of history. Man is determined by the historical, economic, and social conditions, by his *milieu*, and that not only with regard to his fate, but also with regard to his thoughts and volitions and his morality. All this is at bottom nothing but fate, and man himself is not a stable and constant person. What is constant is only his bodily nature with its impulses and passions, its striving for earthly welfare. Man was understood as coming out of a past on which the present depends. But the past is not *his* past, strictly speaking, qualifying him in his genuine self, which he can appropriate as his past and from which he can distance himself. His present goes into a future which, strictly speaking, is not *his* future, for which he can make himself open, or against which he can close himself and for which he is responsible. Therefore it must be said : a genuine self seems not to exist at all. But if it is an indelible urge of human nature to be a real self, to gain 'true existence', then it seems that man is thrown into complete helplessness, into despair.

In the most recent Realism the real self seems to be detected in so far as a reality of life is unveiled which lies beneath the external events and occurrences, and which, as the whole of the personal life, is present in every occasional moment. But we must ask : is historicity so understood, the genuine complete historicity ? Or does there not belong to this what Idealism has taken over from the Christian tradition, namely, the will of man who apprehends responsibility for himself ? The responsibility for the past as *my* past and for the future as *my* future ? According to the Biblical understanding of man responsibility for the past leads to the consciousness of being guilty before God, and responsibility for the future is to be taken upon one as an open readiness over against all that the future brings, gives, and demands.

VIII

THE NATURE OF HISTORY (A)

The Problem of Hermeneutics (The Interpretation of History). The Question of the Objectivity of Historical Knowledge.

(1) WE have not yet raised a question which was not felt as a problem in the interpretations of history we have reviewed, although it is a question which should be discussed first. It is the so-called *hermeneutic question* of how to understand historical documents delivered by tradition. They must be understood, if we want to use them, to reconstruct a picture of the historical past. They must speak to us. In fact, every interpretation of history presupposes a hermeneutic method. This holds for the interpretation of history by the Enlightenment as well as by Hegel or by Marx, or by Toynbee. But usually the historians do not reflect upon this presupposition. In our time the hermeneutic question has come to the fore. In the discussion about the essence and meaning of history there was bound to come to light the problem of how it is possible to know history, whether indeed it is possible to attain objective knowledge of history at all. This second question can only be answered when we have first found an answer to the hermeneutic question : what is the character of historical knowledge ?[1]

[1] Cf. my essay 'Das Problem der Hermeneutik' in *Zeitschrift für Theologie und Kirche* (1950), pp. 47-69 ; reprint in *Glauben und Verstehen*, ii. (1952), pp. 211-35. Cf. also Joachim Wach, *Das Verstehen. Grundzüge einer Geschichte der hermeneutischen Theorie im 19. Jahrhundert*, i-iii (1926. 29. 33.) Emilio Betti, *Zur Grundlegung einer allgemeinen Ausegungslehre* (1954).

The question about the understanding of history can be specialised as the question about the interpretation of literary documents of the past. In this form it is an old question which has played a rôle in philology since Aristotle, and also in jurisprudence. Philology has developed hermeneutic rules. Aristotle already saw that the interpreter has to analyse the structure of a literary document ; he has to understand the details from the whole, and the whole from the details. This is the so-called hermeneutic circle. When the matter in question is a text in a foreign language, then the interpretation has to be according to the grammatical rules of that language. Further the individual usage of language and the style of an author has to be studied as well as the usage of the time. The latter depends on the historical situation ; therefore the knowledge of place and time and culture is also a presupposition of interpretation.

Schleiermacher (1768–1834) already recognised that such hermeneutic rules are not sufficient for the real understanding of a text. He demands the completing of the philological interpretation by a psychological one, and he calls it an interpretation by divination. A literary work has to be understood as a moment in the author's life. The interpreter must reproduce in himself the incident out of which the work which he has to interpret grew. He must, so to speak, produce the work again. Schleiermacher thinks that this is possible because the author and the interpreter share in the same human nature. Everyone has an 'Empfänglichkeit' (suscept-ibility) for all others, and therefore he can understand what others have said.

Schleiermacher's view was continued and taken further by *W. Dilthey* (1833–1911). The art of interpretation was extended by him to other than literary documents, to the documents of art and music for instance. He calls all such documents 'firmly established utterances of life'. The interpreter has to ask for the psychological life which expresses itself in documents which are given and perceived by the senses. That is possible because 'nothing can appear in an individual utterance of some other personality which is not contained in the perceiving vitality'. For 'all individual differences are in the last resort the result not of qualitative differences of the personalities, but only of differences of degree in their psychological accidents'.

We must ask whether this definition of hermeneutic is sufficient. It seems to be obvious with regard to the interpretation of works of art or of religious or philosophical texts. But when I have to understand a mathematical or astronomical or medical text, is it necessary then that I imaginatively put myself into the particular frame of mind of the author ? Is it not my task to repeat or to think again simply the mathematical or astronomical or medical thoughts of the texts ? Or when I have to understand historical-chronological documents, for example the Egyptian or Babylonian inscriptions recording the deeds of war of the rulers, or the famous *Res Gestae Divi Augusti*,[1] is it necessary that I reproduce again the psychological events which occurred in the soul of the authors ? It is obvious that I need only have a certain knowledge of military and political affairs in order to understand such texts. Certainly, it is also possible to read such documents with a different interest, as is shown by G. Misch in his *History of Autobiography*,[2] in that the feeling for life and understanding of the world

[1] See above, p. 5.
[2] Georg Misch, *Geschichte der Autobiographie*, i.

of a certain time and culture finds its expression un-intentionally in such documents.

Hence it is evident that each interpretation is guided by a certain interest, by a certain *putting of the question* : What is my interest in interpreting the documents ? Which question directs me to approach the text ? It is evident that the questioning arises from a particular interest in the matter referred to, and therefore that a particular understanding of the matter is presupposed. I like to call this a *pre-understanding*.

Dilthey is right in saying that there must be a connection between the author and the interpreter, and he sees this connection in the relationship of the psychological life. But if we consider that interpretation must always be guided by a preceding understanding of the matter in question, then we should rather say : the possibility of understanding has its ground in the fact that the interpreter has an actual relation ('Lebensverhältnis') to the matter which finds its expression in the documents, be it directly or indirectly. I suppose this will be clear if we consider how knowledge of a foreign language is to be gained. That happens when the matters, the things, the actions which are designated by foreign words are known to the interpreter by use and intercourse in life. A foreign word designating a thing or an action which is absolutely unknown in my own life, cannot be translated but only picked up as a foreign word. For instance, the German word for window, 'Fenster', is the Latin *fenestra* ; for the old Germans did not use windows or know about them. In such a way also each child learns to understand and to speak words at the same time as he becomes familiar with his surroundings, with its objects, and their use. The condition of all interpretation, therefore, is the simple fact that author and interpreter are living in the same historical world, in which human life is enacted as a life in surroundings, in the knowing use of objects and the intercourse of men. To this naturally belong also the common interests and questions, the problems, the struggles, the passions, and the joys.

I have said that the interest in a certain matter gives the reason for interpretation because from this interest the putting of the question arises. I will now show by a few examples how different questions may arise. The interest may be that of an historical scholar. He will reconstruct the continuity of past history and his special interest may be the political history or the history of the social problems and forms, or the history of mind and of universal culture. In those cases the interpretation will always be determined or at least influenced by his conception of history and of the matters referred to. Or the interest may be that of a psychologist. He subjects the texts to questions of the psychology either of the individual or of the nations or masses. Or he seeks for the psychology of religion, of poetry, of technics, and so on. He is always guided by his pre-understanding of soul and psychical phenomena in general. The interest may be that of aesthetics. The texts or the works of art are analysed formally and asked for their structure. The interpreter is guided by his pre-understanding of beauty or even of the essence of art. Perhaps he is satisfied with a stylistic analysis, perhaps he asks for the psychological incident which expresses itself in the work of art. In every case he is led by his pre-understanding and the conceptions deriving from it.

Finally the interest may be to understand history not in its empirical course but as the sphere of life within which the human being moves, within which human life gains and develops its possibilities. Or briefly stated the interest may be the knowledge of man, as he is and was and ever shall be. In this case the interpreter, reflecting on history, reflects at the same time on his own possibilities and endeavours to gain self-knowledge. His question, then, is the question about human life as his own life which he endeavours to know and at the same time to show to other men. This questioning is only possible, if the interpreter himself is moved by the question about his own existence. And then a certain knowledge of human existence is presupposed, perhaps a very vague and indistinct one, which guides him in putting the questions to which he hopes to find an answer.

If it is true that every interpretation, every questioning and understanding is guided by a pre-understanding, then the question arises whether it is possible to gain objective historical knowledge at all. To this question we now turn.

(2) Certainly, as a rule, the subjectivity of the historian colours his picture of history. It depends, for instance, on the ideal which a historian has of his country and on his image of its future, how he describes its history, how he judges the importance of events, how he estimates the greatness of historical persons, how he distributes worth and worthlessness. According to their different values, different pictures will be produced by a nationalist or a socialist, an idealist or a materialist, a conservative or a liberal. And therefore the portraits of Luther or Goethe, of Napoleon or Bismarck vary in history. Or we may remember the completely subjective picture which Gibbon gives of the decay of the ancient culture.

So far as such pictures are the result of unconcealed

bias and partisanship, we do not need to take account of them, for instance those of the Nazis or the Russian communists. Our question is, whether genuine historical science can attain objectivity. And on the first impression it seems that it may be possible, for it seems true that the events and actions of the past are fixed by the historical documents. Indeed, strict methodical research can recognise objectively a certain part of the historical process, namely, events in so far as they are nothing but occurrences which happened at a certain place in space and time. It is possible, for instance, to fix objectively the fact and the time at which Socrates drank the cup of hemlock, the fact and the time when Caesar crossed the Rubicon, the fact and the time when Luther affixed his ninety-five theses to the doors of the Castle-Church of Wittenberg, or to know objectively the fact that and the time when a certain battle was fought or a certain empire was founded or a certain catastrophe happened. With regard to this it is no real objection to say that in many cases the certainty of historical statements is only a relative one. Of course, there are many events which cannot be fixed because the evidence is not sufficient or not clear, and also the sagacity and the ability of every historian have their limits. But that has no systematic importance ; for in principle, methodical historical research can attain objective knowledge in this sphere.

But we must ask whether history is sufficiently seen when it is only seen as a field of such events and actions as can be fixed in space and time. I do not think so. For at the least history is a movement, a process, in which the single events are not without connection but are connected by the chain of cause and effect. Such connection presupposes powers at work in the historical process. It is not difficult to become aware of such powers. Thucydides already knew how human impulses and passions are moving powers, especially the striving for power and the ambition of individuals and groups. Furthermore, everyone knows how economic and social needs and distresses are factors in the historical process, but that is also true of ideas and ideals. Of course, the understanding and appreciation and valuation of such factors is different, and there is no court which can give a final judgment.

Finally, a historical event or action as historical includes its meaning or importance. What is the importance of the fact that Socrates drank the cup of hemlock ; the importance for the history of Athens ; even for the history of the human mind ? What is the importance of the fact that Caesar crossed the Rubicon ; the importance for the history of Rome ; even of the West ? What is the importance of the fact that Luther affixed his theses to the Church doors ; the importance for the political as well as for the religious history of the following generations ? And is it not the case that the judgment of importance depends on the subjective point of view of the historian ?

Does it follow from all this that it is impossible to attain objective historical knowledge ? Well, that would be so, if objectivity in historical science had the same sense as objectivity in natural science. But we must distinguish between two points of view in historiography so that we may recognise what objectivity in historical science means. The first is, as I may call it, the perspective or viewpoint, chosen by the historian ; the second is, as I like to call it, the existential encounter with history.

First I will try to explain *the question of perspective or viewpoint*. Each historical phenomenon can be seen from different points of view, because man is a complex being. He consists of body and soul, or if one prefers, of body, soul, and mind. He has appetites and passions, he feels physical and spiritual needs, he has will and imagination. He is a political and social being, and he is also an individual with his own peculiarity, and therefore human community can be understood not only as political and social but also as personal relationship. In consequence it is possible to write history as political history as well as economic history, as history of problems and ideas as well as history of individuals and personalities. The historical judgment may be guided by psychological or ethical interest and also by aesthetic interest. Each of these different views is open to one side of the historical process, and from each viewpoint something objectively true will appear. The picture is falsified only if one single viewpoint is made an absolute one, if it comes to be a dogma.

Historiography begins, once the chronicles and novels are left behind, with the interest in political history, for the course of history first comes into consciousness through political changes. Then, in reaction, other views become prevalent and histories of ideas and of economics arise. Lastly modern historians often try to combine the different views and to build up a universal history of human culture or civilisation. In fact, the different historians are usually guided by special interests and questions and that does not matter provided that this question and this point of view do not become absolute, and if the historian is conscious that he sees and shows the phenomenon from a special viewpoint and that it must also be seen from other viewpoints.

Truth becomes manifest objectively to each viewpoint. The subjectivity of the historian does not mean that he sees wrongly, but that he has chosen a special viewpoint, that his research starts with a special question. And we must remember that it is impossible to trace out a historical picture without any question, and that it is possible to perceive a historical phenomenon only from a special point of view. To this extent the subjectivity of the historian is a necessary factor of objective historical knowledge.

But we must reflect on a further point. The subjectivity of the historian goes further than simply choosing a special viewpoint for his research. Already in choosing a viewpoint there is at work what I may call the existential encounter with history.[1] History gains meaning only when the historian himself stands within history and takes part in history. As R. G. Collingwood says : the object of historical knowledge is 'not a mere object, something outside the mind which knows it : it is an activity of thought, which can be known only in so far as the knowing mind re-enacts it and knows itself as so doing. To the historian, the activities whose history he is studying are not spectacles to be watched, but experiences to be lived through in his own mind ; they are objective, or known to him, only because they are also subjective, or activities of his own.'[2] In the same sense Erich Frank says : 'The object of historical understanding is not a thing in itself independent of the mind which contemplates it'. 'In the field of science we have to do with an object which is essentially different from ourselves : we think, but nature does not. The object of historical knowledge is man himself in his subjective nature. In this sphere an ulti-

[1] See my essay 'Wissenschaft und Existenz' in *Ehrfurcht vor dem Leben* (Festschrift zum 80. Geburtstag Albert Schweitzers (1954), pp. 30-43).   [2] R. G. Collingwood, *The Idea of History*, p. 218.

mate distinction between the knower and his object cannot be maintained.'[1]

This does not mean that the historian ascribes a meaning according to his own liking to the historical phenomenon. But it means that historical phenomena are not what they are in pure individual isolation, but only in their relation to the future for which they have importance. We may say : To each historical phenomenon belongs its future, a future in which alone it will appear as that which it really is — to speak precisely we must say : the future in which it evermore appears as that which it is. For ultimately it will show itself in its very essence only when history has reached its end.

Therefore we can understand that the question of meaning in history was raised and answered for the first time within an outlook which believed it knew the end of history. This occurred in the Jewish-Christian understanding of history which was dependent on eschatology.[2] The Greeks did not raise the question of meaning in history and the ancient philosophers had not developed a philosophy of history.[3] A philosophy of history grew up for the first time in Christian thinking, for Christians believed they knew of the end of the world and of history. In modern times the Christian eschatology was secularised by Hegel and by Marx.[4] Hegel and Marx, each in his own way, believed they knew the goal of history and interpreted the course of history in the light of this presupposed goal.

Today we cannot claim to know the end and the goal of history. Therefore the question of meaning in history has become meaningless. But there still re-

[1] Erich Frank, *Philosophical Understanding and Religious Truth*, p. 117, and p. 133, n. 2.   [2] See above, p. 18 ff.
     [3] See above, p. 14 ff.   [4] See above, p. 164 ff.

mains the question of the meaning of single historical phenomena and single historical epochs. To speak more exactly : there remains the question of the importance of single historical events and deeds of our past for our present, a present which is charged with responsibility for our future. For instance : what is the meaning and importance of the decay of the uniform medieval culture in face of the problem of the relationship of the Christian denominations, especially with regard to education ? Or what is the meaning and importance of the French Revolution in view of the problem of the organisation and authority of the state ? Or what is the meaning and importance of the rise of capitalism and socialism in face of the problem of economic organisation ? and so on. In all these cases the analysis of motives and consequences gives light for the demands of our future. The judgment on the past and on the present belong together, and each is clarified by the other.

It is by such historical reflection that the phenomena of the past become real historical phenomena and begin to reveal their meaning. I say they begin — that is to say, objectivity of historical knowledge is not attainable in the sense of absolute ultimate knowledge, nor in the sense that the phenomena could be known in their very 'being in themselves' which the historian could perceive in pure receptivity. This 'being in itself' is an illusion of an objectivising type of thinking which is proper in natural science but not in history.

I must repeat : this does not mean that historical knowledge is subjective in the sense that it depends on the individual desire or pleasure of the subject. On the contrary : the genuine historical question grows out of the historical emotion of the subject, of the person, who feels his responsibility. Therefore historical research includes the readiness to hear the claim which meets one in the historical phenomena. And just for this reason the demand for freedom from presuppositions, for an unprejudiced approach, which is valid for all science, is also valid for historical research. The historian is certainly not allowed to presuppose the results of his research, and he is obliged to keep back, to reduce to silence, his personal desires with regard to these results. But this in no way means that he must annihilate his personal individuality. On the contrary : genuine historical knowledge demands a very personal aliveness of the understanding subject, the very rich unfolding of his individuality. Only the historian who is excited by his participation in history (and that means — who is open for the historical phenomena through his sense of responsibility for the future), only he will be able to understand history. In this sense the most subjective interpretation of history is at the same time the most objective. Only the historian who is excited by his own historical existence will be able to hear the claim of history.

It is in this sense that R. G. Collingwood says that 'historical inquiry reveals to the historian the powers of his own mind'.[1] 'History is thus the self-knowledge of the living mind. For even when the events which the historian studies are events that happened in the distant past, the condition of their being historically known is that they should "vibrate in the historian's mind".'[2] But about Collingwood we have to speak in the next lecture.

[1] l.c. p. 218.   [2] l.c. p. 202.

THE NATURE OF HISTORY (B)

History and Human Existence. Dilthey, Croce, and Jaspers. R. G. Collingwood.

OUR subject 'History and Human Existence' was already treated in the preceding lecture ; our present lecture does not simply continue what we have said, but begins anew. The intention is to proceed to our goal from different starting-points. Here we will consider the thought of some recent philosophers.

(1) It is impossible to treat completely the German authors who engaged in philosophy of history, as for instance, Georg Simmel, Ernst Troeltsch, Friedrich Meinecke.[1] In Germany the question of history was handled with special energy by *Wilhelm Dilthey*. Like other philosophers of his time, Wilhelm Windelband and Heinrich Rickert for instance, he endeavoured to distinguish between historical science and natural science. This is made especially clear by his distinction between explanatory- and understanding-psychology. Whereas explanatory-psychology conceived the psychical life as pure causal sequences, understanding-psychology endeavours to understand psychical life by analysing the meaningful structure of psychical experiences. Psychical

[1] Cf. the excellent review of Fritz Kaufmann, *Geschichtsphilosophie der Gegenwart* (Philosoph. Forschungsberichte, 10) (1931). See also the chapter about the philosophy of the twentieth century with which Heinz Heimsoeth has completed the *Lehrbuch der Geschichte der Philosophie* of Wilhelm Windelband (1935).

life expresses and objectivises itself in productions, in works, which are each a closed whole of meaning. Human life is not subject to neutral consideration as pure object, as are natural phenomena, but has its own vitality, the manifestations of which are in themselves full of aim and meaning. History, therefore, is the field in which these manifestations take shape in the works of culture, in social and political orders as well as in philosophy, religion, world-views ('Weltanschauung'), and in art and poetry. Every work is a manifestation of psychical life. What we experience and remember as the fruit of our experiences expresses itself and forms itself into the meaningful unity of a work.

Historical science, therefore, is the interpretation of such works. It has the task of understanding the objectifications of life by reducing them, so to speak, to the ground from which they grew, namely, to the ground of the creative life of the soul which reveals itself only in its objectifications. Such understanding is possible, as we have tried to show in the preceding lecture, because the interpreter shares in general human nature. The distance between the interpreted object and the interpreting subject vanishes, for they are both united by virtue of the soul which lives in both of them. Objectifications of soul can be understood by living souls.

Of course, there are different types of psychical experience and therefore different types of philosophies, religions, and world-views. But they are all expressions or manifestations of psychical life, of the living soul. The historian, therefore, is not interested in raising the question of truth, but has only to ask for revelation of soul. As Dilthey says : 'We are seeking the soul. That is the end at which we have arrived after the long development of historiography.'

Certainly, there may be something like evolution in history but not in the sense of an advancing improvement. There is evolution in so far as human life is temporal life, subjected to time. No one shaping of life is ultimately conclusive. Therefore no other definition of man's being can be made except that man is a living soul. His life is historical life ; that means : the soul lives in constantly creating new works as manifestations of itself.

It is clear that this conception of history does not have any eschatology. Perhaps it may be said that eschatological perfection is, so to speak, distributed among the several moments of the psychical experiences from which each work originates, and that these moments recur in the understanding soul. That may be called eschatology transformed into aestheticism. It seems to me, indeed, that Dilthey looks at history principally from an aesthetic standpoint as at a spectacle which the historian enjoys in perceiving all the different possibilities of the human being as his own.

This conception of history avoids relativism and nihilism only in that Dilthey sees the ground and origin of all relativities in the life of the soul which reveals itself mysteriously in its manifestations. But whoever asks for truth is left in embarrassment, and this gives rise to the criticism of Dilthey by Collingwood. But to prepare ourselves for Collingwood we will have a look at Croce and Jaspers.

(2) *Benedetto Croce* starts from the problem of Historicism.[1] Historicism, he says, is the conviction that life and reality are history and nothing but history. He overcomes the relativism of historicism by radicalising

[1] See primarily his comprehensive work *History as the Story of Liberty* (1941) (the Italian original, 1938).

it. The relativity of historical phenomena gains in his thought a positive meaning, for he understands history as the process of the developing mind. 'To interpret and value a single work among other works means at the same time to conceive this work within the unity of the process which is composed by them all. It is, therefore, connected with the whole and stands in definite relations to the other works which precede and follow it.' The consequence of this is the paradoxical statement that historical truth and therefore the whole of truth lies in the knowledge of the single individual.

That sounds like Hegel. Indeed, Croce is following Hegel, but he modifies his conception in a decisive manner. For Croce, as for Hegel, history is, as history of mind, history of freedom. History is a continuous creation of life, a 'continuous growing of mind beyond itself in such a manner that nothing created disappears and nothing remains standing firm, but there is a continuous growth'. But this is not what Hegel believes. For Hegel understands the historical process as a process embracing the origin of history, its growth to maturity, and its ultimate fixation in its last stage. He therefore understands the historical process as progress. According to Croce there is no progress in the sense of Hegel. On the contrary, the paradox is valid that humanity persists as the same through all changes. 'Humanity is a whole within each epoch and in each human individual.' The whole of humanity 'exists only in its actions, but the actions are not actions in general, but definite historical tasks or problems. Humanity becomes completed in performing those tasks ; and in ever again meeting new tasks it completes itself over and over again as a whole.' Croce makes no claim to understand the past from the presupposed end of history, but remains within history.

Every present moment, however related to the whole historical process, is full of meaning, for the meaning of the whole process is concentrated in the now, in the present moment.

Croce is therefore not interested in knowing history in its completeness ; for historical truth lies in the individual phenomenon in which over and over again the whole is present. But in another sense historical process is a progress in so far as every present moment has to take up the heritage of its past in developing the problems and solving the tasks which grow out of that past. And every present hour is responsible for its future. In this progress the historian himself has his place, for it is his task to know the meaning of every individual phenomenon within the nexus of the whole and to renew and revive the problems out of which it grew, by a kind of Platonic 'anamnesis' (remembering). History is the history of mind. Therefore historical knowledge is at the same time self-knowledge and knowledge of mind. All knowledge of truth is ultimately historical knowledge. Therefore historical science and philosophy coincide.

It is clear that according to Croce there is no eschatology — neither religious nor secularised eschatology. Paradoxically it may be said that Croce identifies history and eschatology, because he ascribes to every present
· moment in the historical process the fullness of the whole of history.

When we compare Dilthey and Croce, we can state that both of them draw the consequence of historicism, namely, that the historian himself stands within history and partakes of it. He cannot take a stand outside history at an 'Archimedean point'. Both of them agree in the conviction that it is senseless to ask for knowledge of universal world-history in its entirety, as though from such knowledge the meaning in history could be discovered. For such an enterprise a stand-point outside of history would be the presupposition. Both of them avoid relativism and nihilism ; Dilthey by his belief in the life of the soul which becomes manifest in all historical phenomena ; Croce by his belief in the mind which according to him is essentially reason. To this difference their difference in understanding history corresponds. For Dilthey the understanding of history is an event of experience, for Croce an act of knowledge. Certainly, for both of them to understand history means to revive the past in the present, but in a totally different way ; for Dilthey, by reproducing past psychical experiences by imagination ; for Croce, by taking over the problems and tasks of the past. For both of them the whole field of history is at the disposal of historical research and knowledge, but there is no interest in elaborating this field as a whole or in taking up each epoch as an object of research without selection. The traditional division of history into epochs therefore becomes unimportant for Croce, though it may have a certain value as a study preliminary to genuine historical knowledge. The choice of the field of research is regulated, according to Croce, by the present interest ; for historical knowledge is demanded at every time by the necessity of action in the present.[1] The problems of the present open men's eyes for the problems of history. It is for this reason that the historian himself stands within history and partakes in it.

Certainly, Croce has overcome the negative consequences of historicism, whereas for Dilthey the worrying question of truth remains without an answer. But

[1] See also the important essay of Fritz Kaufmann, *Reality and Truth in History* (Perspectives in Philosophy (1953)), p. 46 f.

we may ask whether the solution of the problem by Croce does justice to the true essence of the individual. Is it sufficient to say, as he does, that 'reason is the very essence of man' ? Or is Dilthey's conception of soul in this respect superior ? We shall return to this question later.

(3) We can say only a little about the book of *Karl Jaspers* on the origin and meaning of history,[1] but we must briefly mention him as a counterpart to Dilthey and especially to Croce. He does not start from the problem of historicism nor, as far as I understand him, has he recognised the historicity of man in its radicality. He asks for the meaning of history, and he thinks we must discover this meaning by surveying the whole of human history in its totality. Hence his seeking for the origin of history, his curious interest in prehistoric times, and his endeavour to show the structure of world-history. Hence his strange theory of the 'Achsenzeit' (time of the axis) on which universal history is established ; that is the time about 500 B.C. within which, from 800 till 200, the process took place in which—after the old high cultures in the 'Zweistromland' (land of the two rivers), in Egypt, on the Indus, and in China—'man became conscious of the being as a whole, of himself and his limits'; and so occurred the breaking through to 'the principles of the human being in the "Grenz-situationen" (boundary-situations) which are valid till today'. Hence finally his analysis of the present epoch of science and technics and the prognosis of the future.

It seems to me that Jaspers claims to have attained a stand-point as a philosopher outside of history, although his utterances in this regard are not always clear. But it is clear that he seeks for the individual a stand-point

[1] Karl Jaspers, *Vom Ursprung und Ziel der Geschichte* (1949).

beyond history in what he calls 'Transzendenz' (transcendence) or in the origin of all being or ground of being. It seems to me that what is right in this endeavour lies in the feeling that the very essence of the human individual is not fully understood in such philosophies as that of Croce, but I cannot see that his attempt is brought to clear expression. It is clear, however, that Jaspers endeavours to understand history as the history of men who are responsible for the future, and he gives an analysis of our present time with its threatening problems in order to make the responsibility urgently felt. This stress upon responsibility also shows, as it seems to me, that Jaspers strives to overcome the relativism of historicism, but it is regrettable that he refuses to discuss this problem explicitly with other philosophers.

(4) The best that is said about the problems of history is, in my view, contained in the book of R. G. Collingwood, *The Idea of History* (1946, 1949). In this title 'History' means historical science, historical research, or inquiry; but, in the consideration of what history in this sense is, naturally the idea of history in the sense of the historical events must indirectly become clear.

According to Collingwood, the object of history (as historical science) is the 'actions of human beings that have been done in the past' (p. 9). Or he says : 'all history properly so called is the history of human affairs' (p. 212). Throughout his book runs the attempt to elucidate the distinction between historical and natural science and their objects. The objects of historical science are, as I have said, the actions of men. Every event has an outside and an inside. The work of the historian 'may begin by discovering the outside of an event, but it can never end there; he must always remember that the event was an action, and that his main task is to think himself into this action, to discern the thought of its agent' (p. 213). For thoughts are the inside of actions, and the historical process is a 'process of thoughts'. The historian cannot *perceive* the thoughts as a scientist perceives natural facts, but he must *understand* them by *re-enacting the process of thought*. History, therefore, is re-enactment of the thoughts of the past in the historian's mind. As a process of thought the historical process is the life of the mind, and therefore the knowledge of history is at the same time self-knowledge ; it is 'the self-knowledge of the historian's own mind as the present revival and reliving of past experiences' (p. 175).

It is clear that the re-enacting of past thoughts is by no means a simple reproduction or repetition of past thoughts 'in its immediacy as the unique act of thought with its unique context in the life of an individual thinker. . . . It is the act of thought itself, in its survival and revival at different times and in different persons : once in the historian's own life, once in the life of the person whose history he is narrating' (p. 303). That means : the re-enactment of past thoughts is an autonomous critical act of re-thinking. The re-enactment 'is not a passive surrender to the spell of another's mind ; it is a labour of active and therefore critical thinking. . . . This criticism of the thought whose history he (the historian) traces is not something secondary to tracing the history of it. It is an indispensable condition of the historical knowledge itself' (p. 215). This criticism is not made from a stand-point outside of history but within history. If the systems of thought of the past 'remain valuable to posterity, that is not in spite of their strictly historical character but because of it. To us, the ideas expressed in them are ideas belonging to the past ; but it is not a dead past ; by understanding it historically we incorporate it into our present thought, and enable ourselves by developing and criticising it to use that heritage for our own advancement' (p. 230).

'The historical process is itself a process of thought, and it exists only in so far as the minds which are parts of it know themselves for parts of it. By historical thinking, the mind, whose self-knowledge is history, not only discovers within itself those powers of which historical thought reveals the possession, but actually develops those powers from a latent to an actual state, brings them into effective existence' (p. 226). 'Whenever he (the historian) finds certain historical matters unintelligible, he has discovered a limitation of his own mind' (p. 218). It is in this sense that it is true : 'Die Weltgeschichte ist das Weltgericht', for 'it is the historian himself who stands at the bar of judgment, and there reveals his own mind in its strength and weakness, its virtues and its vices' (p. 219). This becomes clearer when we consider what Collingwood thinks about the objectivity of historical knowledge or about evidence.

Genuine historical knowledge does not rely on statements but only on evidence, and the last piece of evidence is the present of the historian from which the questions spring, which open up the view into the past. 'Every present has a past of its own, and any imaginative reconstruction aims at reconstructing the past of this present, the present in which the act of imagination is going on, as here and now perceived. In principle the aim of any such act is to use the entire perceptible here-and-now as evidence for the entire past through whose process it has come into being' (p. 247). 'For even when the events which the historian studies are events that happened in the distant past, the condition of their being historically known is that they should "vibrate in the historian's mind", that is to say, that the evidence for them should be here and now before him and intelligible for him' (p. 202).

Therefore the relation of subject and object which is characteristic for natural science has no value for historical science. Historical science is objective precisely in its subjectivity, because the subject and object of historical science do not exist independently of one another. In this sense Collingwood says : 'The historian's thought must spring from the organic unity of his total experience, and be a function of his entire personality with its practical as well as its theoretical interests' (p. 305). In German we could say : historical knowledge is 'existential' knowledge, as I have tried to show in the preceding lecture.[1]

From this it follows that historical knowledge is itself a historical event or a stage of the historical process within which the historian himself is interwoven as well as the object which he endeavours to know. Therefore the results of his research are not ultimate statements. 'The historian, however long and faithfully he works, can never say that his work, even in crudest outlines or in this or that smallest detail, is done once for all' (p. 248 f.). 'Every new generation must rewrite history in its own way ; every new historian, not content with giving new answers to old questions, must revise the questions themselves' (p. 248).

There is no end or goal in the process of historical knowledge, any more than in the process of history itself. Collingwood does not know any eschatology and he cannot foresee the future, he is not a prophet. 'History (in the sense of historical knowledge) must end with the present' (p. 120). But that does not mean that

[1] See above, pp. 119-122.

there is no progress. On the contrary, progress is an essential characteristic of the process of history. But progress must not be confounded with evolution. 'Historical progress is only another name for activity itself, as a succession of acts each of which arises out of the last . . . the accomplished act gives rise to a new problem' (p. 324). 'Any past experience lives in the mind of the historian, as a past experience known as past . . . but re-enacted here and now together with a development of itself that is partly constructive or positive and partly critical or negative' (p. 334).

From this stand-point an answer can be given to the question : 'Why history ? What is history for ?'; history in these questions means, of course, historical knowledge or science. Collingwood says : 'My answer is that history is "for" human self-knowledge. . . . The value of history, then, is that it teaches us what man has done and thus what man is' (p. 10).[1] And what is man ? The answer must be : man is essentially mind. Mind, however, is not a substance, not something lying behind its activities. 'Any study of mind is a study of its activities' (p. 221). 'In the case of a machine, we distinguish structure from function', but that is impossible with regard to mind (p. 221). 'History does not presuppose mind ; it is the life of mind itself, which is not mind except so far as it both lives in historical process and knows itself as so living' (p. 227).

Collingwood conceives the full historicity of the human being as radically as Croce. But there is a difference. For Collingwood mind is not simply reason, although there is no mind without reason. But mind is something more than mere reason. Collingwood recog-

[1] For these questions, see also Fritz Kaufmann, *Reality and Truth in History* (Perspectives in Philosophy (1953)), p. 49.

nises the unity of will and thinking in defining thought as 'reflective thought' or as 'reflective effort, the effort to do something of which we have a conception before we do it' (p. 308). Or he defines the 'reflective or deliberate act' as 'an act which we not only do, but intend to do before doing it' (p. 309). 'Reflective acts may be roughly described as the acts which we do on purpose' (p. 309). To judge an action of a person means to judge it 'by reference to his intention' (p. 309). It seems to be clear that, according to Collingwood, the conception of thought includes the sense of intention and purpose. I remind you of the words, already cited : 'The historian's thought must spring from the organic unity of his total experience, and be a function of his entire personality with its practical as well as its theoretical interests' (p. 305). From all this it follows that Collingwood conceives thought not as a mere act of thinking, but as an act of man in his entire existence, as an act of decision.

To sum up. Collingwood as well as Croce is aware of the historicity of the human being, and, like Croce, he avoids the consequence of relativism and nihilism. For every *now*, every moment, in its historical related-ness of course, has within itself a full meaning. The past from which every present springs is not a determining past, but a past offering to the present the problems which demand solution or development. In knowing his situation the individual knows himself. Therefore the present is meaningful for the individual. Of course, to ask for meaning in history is not allowable if one is asking for meaning in the sense of goal. The meaning in history is immanent in history, because history is the history of mind. And therefore it may be said, as we said of Croce, that for Collingwood every present moment is an eschatological moment, and that history and eschatology are identified.

It seems to me, however, that the meaning of mind and of self-knowledge should be understood a little more profoundly than Collingwood has done. His answer to the question : why history ? is, as we have seen : history is for human self-knowledge. But what is the answer when we ask : why self-knowledge ? Certainly, for Collingwood self-knowledge includes the knowledge of the present situation with its heritage and its problems. But, must we not then say : self-knowledge is consciousness of responsibility over against the future ? And the act of self-knowledge, is it not at the same time an act of decision ? I do not think that I am really contradicting Collingwood. For since, according to him, thought includes purpose or intention, then it follows that self-knowledge cannot be a mere theoretical act, but is also an act of decision. If that is true, then the historicity of the human being is completely understood when the human being is understood as living in responsibility over against the future and therefore in decision. And, furthermore, it must be said that historicity in its full sense is not a self-evident natural quality of the human individual, but a possibility which must be grasped and realised. The man who lives without self-knowledge and without consciousness of his responsibility is a historical being in a much lower degree, one who is at the mercy of historical conditions, handing himself over to relativity. Genuine historicity means to live in responsibility and history is a call to historicity.

But let us make still another critical remark about Collingwood. His definition of history as the history of human actions seems to me to be one-sided. For human life goes its way not only through actions, but also through events which encounter us through that which happens to one. And the reactions to these events are also actions in a certain sense. Man is responsible in his reaction too, and his behaviour or conduct in the face of such events is also decision. The problems of the present do not all grow from the historical past, but also from encounters which demand decisions. But about this subject we must say more in the next lecture.

X

CHRISTIAN FAITH AND HISTORY

Christianity and History according to H. Butterfield. The Existentialist Interpretation of History and Eschatology.

(1) WHEN we look back into the history of historiography and the different ways of understanding history we see a many-coloured picture. Indeed, history can be understood as political history as well as economic or social history, as the history of mind or ideas as well as the history of civilisations. All these views are legitimate, but they all are one-sided, and the question is whether there is a core of history from which history ultimately gains its essence and its meaning and becomes relevant. Otherwise it remains a meaningless play or a mere spectacle.

Now we have seen that the question about meaning in history cannot be answered when we ask for the meaning of history as the entire historical process, as though it were like some human undertaking whose meaning we can recognise when we can survey it in its entirety. For meaning in history in this sense could only be recognised if we could stand at the end or goal of history and detect its meaning by looking backwards ; or if we could stand outside history. But man can neither stand at the goal, nor outside of history. He stands within history. The question about meaning in history, however, can be put and must be put in a different sense, namely, as the question about the nature, the essence of history. And this brings us again to the question : What is the core of history ? What is its real subject ?

The answer is : man. We have already seen that this is the answer of Jacob Burckhardt : the historian has to deal with man as he is and was and ever shall be. We have seen, moreover, that Toynbee's valuation of religion leads of itself to the inference that the real subject of history is man. And the understanding of history by Dilthey, by Croce, and by Collingwood points in the same direction. Finally this answer is implicitly contained in the often repeated definition of history as the field of human actions. For to live in actions is the very essence of man.

We usually distinguish between history and nature. The course of both passes within time. But the difference is clear, for history is constituted by human actions. 'Action is distinguished from natural events in so far as it does not merely happen, but has to be expressly performed, borne and animated by some kind of consciousness.'[1] History as the field of human actions cannot, however, be cut off from nature and natural events. Geographical and climatic conditions are relevant for civilisations. The historical character of peoples is, although not determined, nevertheless still influenced by the cold or hot climate, by abundance or scarcity of water, by whether they live inland or on the coast, and so on. Natural events, such as change of climate, can bring about historical movements, such as migrations or wars. The reason for such events can also be the increase of population. And from this point of view even eating and drinking belong indirectly to history, although they are not historical actions, as Collingwood rightly stresses. Particular events in nature, such as natural catastrophes,

[1] Fritz Kaufmann, *Reality and Truth in History*, p. 43.

can also become of historical importance, for instance when they call forth inventions. Or we may remember the thunder-clap which drove Luther into the monastery.

All these conditions and events within nature, so far as they are relevant for human life and history, may be called encounters (in German : 'Widerfahrnisse') in contrast to human actions. Indeed, not only human actions but also human sufferings belong to history ; in a certain sense they are also actions in so far as they are reactions.[1]

(2) Now, when we reflect about human actions and when we consider that human actions are caused by purposes and intentions, then it becomes clear that human life is always directed towards the future. As long as man lives, he is never content with his present, but his intentions, his expectations, his hopes, and his fears are always stretched into the future. He can never, like Goethe's 'Faust', say to the moment : 'Stand still, thou art so beautiful'. That means : the genuine life of man is always before him ; it is always to be apprehended, to be realised. Man is always on the way ; each present hour is questioned and challenged by its future. That means at the same time that the real essence of all that man does and undertakes in his present becomes revealed only in the future as important or vain, as fulfilment or failure. All actions are risks.

But the fact that man can either gain his genuine life or miss it, includes the fact that this very thing which he is really aiming at, genuineness of life, is at the same time demanded from him. His genuine willing is at the same time his being obliged. The realisation of his genuine life stands before him as obligation as well as intention.

[1] See above, p. 137

The good which everyone aims at — as Socrates already saw — is at the same time the ethical law which he has to obey.

The concrete form of the demand is always determined by the present situation. Historicism is perfectly right in seeing that every present situation grows out of the past ; but it misunderstands the determination by the past as purely causal determination and fails to see it as leading into a situation of questions, of problems. It does not understand the present situation as the situation of decision — a decision which, as our decision over against our future, is at the same time our decision over against our past concerning the way in which it is to determine our future. For our past has by no means one meaning only ; it is ambiguous. In consequence of its misunderstanding of the present, historicism also misunderstands the future as determined by the past through causality instead of being open.

The concrete possibilities for human actions are, of course, limited by the situation arising from the past. Not all things are possible just as we wish them at every time. But the future is open in so far as it brings the gain or the loss of our genuine life and thereby gives to our present its character as moment of decision. Historicism in its traditional form overlooks the dangerous character of the present, its character of risk. The relativity of each present moment, rightly seen by historicism, is therefore not relativity in the sense in which any particular point within a causal series is a relative one, but has the positive sense that the present is the moment of decision, and by the decision taken the yield of the past is gathered in and the meaning of the future is chosen. This is the character of every historical situation ; in it the problem and the meaning of past and future are enclosed and are waiting, as it were, to be unveiled by human decisions.

Croce and Collingwood saw rightly that the relativity of every moment and every historical phenomenon has a positive meaning. But, in understanding mind as acting reason, Croce does not take into account what I have called the encounters. According to him, the historian has not to deal with the irrational, with sufferings, catastrophes, and evils, or only in so far as they are occasions, incitements for human activity. But he does not see that reaction is a specific kind of action, that to suffer is not a purely passive kind of behaviour, but that it becomes activity in so far as it means to tolerate, to endure. To this extent it is an evidence of will and belongs to historicity. Croce ignores this because, according to him, the very essence of man is reason, not primary will. But though human will is in general not without reason, the will is to be esteemed as the determining factor, if it is correct that human life is lived through decisions. When Collingwood calls the actions, which the historian has to deal with, thoughts, it is not in the one-sided manner of Croce. As we have seen, thought for him includes purpose and intention ; he recognises the unity of willing and thinking.[1] But he fails to draw all the consequences of his conception. He rightly recognises that history is the history of problems and that every historical situation contains problems whose solution is the task of the responsible present. But, as with Croce, his view is directed only to the problem of actions, not to the problem of encounters, of suffering.

In looking back to Croce and especially to Collingwood we can say that the problem of historicism is solved,

[1] See above, p. 135.

that the embarrassment into which historicism had led is overcome. First, *history is understood as the history of man*. It may well be said that history is the history of mind. But mind is not realised otherwise than in human thoughts, and human thoughts are ultimately intentions of individuals. The subject of history is therefore humanity within the individual human persons ; therefore it may be said : The subject of history is man. Secondly, *the relativity of every historical situation is understood as having a positive meaning*.

Modern historicism, as we have seen, understood the historicity of man in such a way that it saw man bound by the historical conditions of the time in question. In this way it had the merit of awaking anew the question of the meaning of history, for just this question became urgent for the individual who was taught that he is at the mercy of history. Historicism has also the merit of itself showing the way in which it is to be overcome. It has destroyed by implication the conception of the relation between historian and history as the relation between subject and object. The historian cannot see history from a neutral stand-point outside history. His seeing of history is itself a historical event. So historicism prepared the way for the deeper conception of historicity developed by Croce and Collingwood. Historicity now gains the meaning of responsibility over against the future, which is at the same time the responsibility over against the heritage of the past in face of the future. Historicity is the nature of man who can never possess his genuine life in any present moment, but is always on the way and yet is not at the mercy of a course of history independent of himself. Every moment is the *now* of responsibility, of decision. From this the unity of history is to be understood. This unity does not consist in a causal connection of events, nor in a progress developing by logical necessity ; for the historical process falls to the responsibility of men, to the decisions of the individual persons. In this responsibility, as responsibility over against the past as well as over against the future, the unity of history is grounded. In this sense it may be said, as Croce did, following the intention of Hegel, that humanity is always a whole in each epoch and in each human being.

(3) But does it follow from this that the entire course of history is a field without heights and depths ? That there are no differences in the historical phenomena, persons, and thoughts ? Are we not allowed to make distinctions, because the Sophists in Athens were human beings as well as Socrates and Plato ? Or Cesare Borgia as well as Luther ? Or an average author as well as Milton or Goethe ? Or because a Gothic cathedral and a railway station in Gothic style are both expressions of human thought ? By no means.

Collingwood states clearly that the re-enactment of past thought is a matter of evaluating and criticising, precisely because of our responsibility.[1] The events of the past cannot be established by neutral perception as facts and events in nature can be. Historical facts and events are not to be perceived but to be understood, and understanding means at the same time evaluating.

But there remains one point which has not yet been considered, at any rate explicitly, either by Croce or by Collingwood. They are right in saying that knowledge of history is at the same time *self-knowledge*. Both of them understand this self-knowledge as the knowledge of oneself as historical and this means the knowledge of one's situation and of the problems, the tasks, and the

[1] See above, pp. 131 ff.

possibilities which are contained within it. This formal definition of self is certainly correct, but I do not think it is sufficient. *The human person* is not completely recognised so long as it is not explicitly taken into account that in the decisions of the individual there is a personal subject, an *I*, which decides and which has its own vitality. This does not mean that the *I* is a mysterious substance beyond or beside the historical life. Life is always within the historical movement; its genuineness stands always before it in the future. But the subject of the ever-new decisions is the same, namely, the *I*, as an ever-growing and becoming, an ever-increasing, improving or degenerating *I*. Signs of this identity of the *I* within the flow of decisions are memory and consciousness and the phenomenon of repentance.

And we may also ask whether the decisions through which life runs are solely decisions demanded by historical situations and historical tasks. Decisions within personal encounters, decisions of friendship and love, or of indifference and hatred — can these be called answers to historical problems? Gratitude or personal fidelity, are they answers to historical problems? Choosing a career of life, prepared by one's gifts and personal encounters, can that be called decision about a historical problem? Certainly, all these decisions and kinds of behaviour may have consequences for history, but they are not in themselves decisions over against historical problems in the sense in which Croce and Collingwood speak about historical problems. Neither are patience and endurance in sufferings or joy in beauty answers to the questions of historical situations. Self-knowledge, arising from one's personal destiny, may concern blessings or distresses or the threatening nearness of death, but is this the same thing as the self-knowledge arising from historical reflection described by Croce and Collingwood?

It seems to me that the self in question has a further dimension which Croce and Collingwood neglect. We may call this the dimension of *Personality*. Its existence is recognised, in my opinion by Dilthey, when he tries to detect the experiences of the soul as the origin of historical works.[1] And this is perhaps also intended by Jaspers when he seeks for the individual a stand-point beyond history.[2] Following the hints of Dilthey, Heidegger says in his analysis of the human being as temporal-historical that the human being chooses its genuine existence by resolution and is thereby brought into the simplicity of its destiny.[3] Butterfield also seems to have personality in mind, but does not see clearly the historicity of the human being.

For it must be stressed that what we call *personality* is also temporal-historical and is constant only as a possibility which is ever to be realised. Personality is not a substance behind the decisions, a substance in relation to which the concrete historical decisions are only accidents. My self-understanding as personality depends on my decisions, which may for the most part be unconscious, made without reflection. As I have already said, the *I* is an ever-growing, ever-becoming, ever-increasing entity. Personality experiences its own history within the frame of universal history and interwoven within it, but nevertheless as a history which has its own meaning and is not merged into universal history.

This is the justification of autobiography, which plays no rôle either in Croce or in Collingwood. In auto-

---

[1] See above, p. 124.   [2] See above, p. 129.
[3] Martin Heidegger, *Sein und Zeit*, p. 394.

biography the author gives an account of the personal history of his life. Certainly, autobiographies may gain an extraordinary importance for universal history as, for instance, the 'Confessions' of Augustine or of Rousseau. But this clearly shows that history has a dimension not included in the concept of it as the history of problems, favoured by Croce and Collingwood. History is also moved by the personal self-understanding of the persons who are acting in history. Such personal self-understanding usually finds its expression in so-called *world-views* ('*Weltanschauungen*') and religions. Therefore history can also be viewed as the history of 'Weltanschauungen', and Dilthey is justified in distinguishing types of 'Weltanschauungen'.

Now there can be no doubt that there is a reciprocal interaction between the so-called 'Weltanschauungen' and the history of problems which Croce and Collingwood have in view, especially between 'Weltanschauung' and science. At the basis of Greek science and philosophy lies a self-understanding of man which is in turn shaped by science. In Greek tragedy this self-understanding is questioned, most of all by Euripides, and it eventually broke down, at any rate for a great mass of people, in Gnosticism. In connection with Gnosticism, and at the same time in opposition to it, Christianity arose.

It seems to me one cannot explain such changes purely from the viewpoint of the history of problems any more than the changes from the Middle Ages to the Renaissance, to the Enlightenment, to Idealism and Romanticism, although in all these changes the history of politics, economics, and science was also relevant. This explanation is impossible because all these 'Weltanschauungen' and religions are permanent possibilities of human self-understanding which once they have found expression in history remain as ever-present possibilities coming to life at different times in different forms. For fundamentally they are not answers to special historical problems in definite historical situations, but are expressions of personal self-understanding, of personality, however they may be stimulated by special historical situations.

But now one may ask whether the consequence is a complete relativism, whether all 'Weltanschauungen' and religions are expressions of possible self-understanding. The question of truth seems to disappear, as, in fact, happens in Dilthey. Naturalistic theories then offer themselves to explain the peculiarities of the different 'Weltanschauungen' and religions by reducing them to geographical and general-historical conditions.

But this conclusion is not justified. From the fact that there are different possibilities of self-understanding it does not follow that they are all equally right. On the contrary, the view of the different possibilities raises the question of legitimate self-understanding. How have I to understand myself? May there not be an inadequate self-understanding? May self-understanding not go astray? Can the risk of human life be escaped by possession of a 'Weltanschauung'?

In fact, the personal history of the individual clearly shows that this history has not always one consistent meaning, one straight direction. It may go through repentance, through doubt, yes, through despair. There are breaks, mistakes, and conversions. A so-called 'Weltanschauung' is genuine when it originates ever anew within changing historical situations and encounters. It cannot become an assured possession as can a result of scientific research. Mostly it is misconceived as scientific theory which can solve all the riddles of life.

But it is then cut off from the ground from which alone it can grow, from the personal life. In this misconception 'Weltanschauung' is in reality a flight from historicity.

But with this we have gained a criterion for a legitimate human self-understanding. A 'Weltanschauung', we may say, is the more legitimated the more it expresses the historicity of the human being. Self-understanding is the more astray the more it fails to appreciate historicity and flees from its own history. Gnostic self-understanding failed in this way and so did Stoicism so far as the Stoic ideal of life was consistently conceived, namely, as the behaviour of the man who shuts himself off from all encounters, good as well as evil, in order to preserve the calm of his interior, and who understands freedom only negatively as being untouched by all encounters, instead of as freedom for responsible acting.

I do not intend to review the different 'Weltanschauungen' to discover in what measure the personality of man and his historicity is understood by them. But there can be no doubt that the radical understanding of the historicity of man has appeared in Christianity, the way being prepared in the Old Testament.[1] This is proved by the fact that real autobiography arose for the first time within Christianity. From this origin the understanding of the human being as historical became effective in the West, and it remained vivid even when it was divorced from Christian faith and secularised as in the modern philosophy of existence which finds its extreme form in Sartre.

(4) But we have to ask : What is the peculiarity of *Christian* faith besides the fact that it understands the

[1] With regard to Paul, see above, p. 43 f. With regard to Augustine, see above, p. 64 f.

human being as historical? Christian faith believes that man does not have the freedom which is presupposed for historical decisions. In fact, I am always determined by my own past by which I have become what I am and of which I cannot get rid, of which in the last resort I am unwilling to be rid, although unconsciously. For everyone refuses to give himself up without reservation. Certainly everyone can be conscious of his responsibility and has a relative freedom in the moments of decision. But if he recognises that this freedom is only a relative one, that means that his freedom is limited by himself as he is coined by his past. Radical freedom would be freedom from himself. The man who understands his historicity radically, that is, the man who radically understands himself as someone future, or in other words, who understands his genuine self as an ever-future one, has to know that his genuine self can only be offered to him as a gift by the future. Usually man strives to dispose over the future. And indeed, his very historicity misleads him to this attempt, because his historicity includes responsibility for the future. His responsibility awakes the illusion of having power of disposal. In this illusion man remains 'the old man', fettered by his past. He does not recognise that only the radically free man can really take over responsibility, and that he is not allowed to look round for guarantees, not even the guarantees of a moral law, which take off or lighten the weight of responsibility, as it is expressed in Luther's famous words : *pecca fortiter*. Man has to be free from himself or to become free from himself. But man cannot get such freedom by his own will and strength, for in such effort he would remain 'the old man' ; he can only receive this freedom as gift.

Christian faith believes that it receives this gift of

freedom, by which man becomes free from himself in order to gain himself. 'Whoever will save his life shall lose it, but whoever will lose his life shall find it.' The truth of this statement is not yet realised when it is only comprehended as general truth. For man cannot say this word to himself, it must be said to him — always individually to you and to me. Just this is the meaning of the Christian message. It does not proclaim the idea of the grace of God as a general idea but addresses and calls man and imparts to him the grace of God which makes him free from himself.

This message knows itself to be legitimated by the revelation of the grace of God in Jesus Christ. According to the New Testament, *Jesus Christ is the eschatological event*, the action of God by which God has set an end to the old world. In the preaching of the Christian Church the eschatological event will ever again become present and does become present ever and again in faith. The old world has reached its end for the believer, he is 'a new creature in Christ'. For the old world has reached its end with the fact that he himself as 'the old man' has reached his end and is now 'a new man', a free man.

It is the paradox of the Christian message that the eschatological event, according to Paul and John,[1] is not to be understood as a dramatic cosmic catastrophe but as happening within history, beginning with the appearance of Jesus Christ and in continuity with this occurring again and again in history, but not as the kind of historical development which can be confirmed by any historian. It becomes an event repeatedly in preaching and faith. Jesus Christ is the eschatological event not as an

[1] For Paul, see above, pp. 45-7, 49. For John, see above, pp. 47-49.

established fact of past time but as repeatedly present, as addressing you and me here and now in preaching.

Preaching is address, and as address it demands answer, *decision*. This decision is obviously something other than the decisions in responsibility over against the future which are demanded in every present moment. For in the decision of faith I do not decide on a responsible action, but on a new understanding of myself as free from myself by the grace of God and as endowed with my new self, and this is at the same time the decision to accept a new life grounded in the grace of God. In making this decision I also decide on a new understanding of my responsible acting. This does not mean that the responsible decision demanded by the historical moment is taken away from me by faith, but it does mean that all responsible decisions are born of love. For love consists in unreservedly being for one's neighbour, and this is possible only for the man who has become free from himself.

It is the paradox of Christian being that the believer is taken out of the world and exists, so to speak, as unworldly and that at the same time he remains within the world, within his historicity. To be historical means to live from the future. The believer too lives from the future; first because his faith and his freedom can never be possession; as belonging to the eschatological event they can never become facts of past time but are reality only over and over again as event; secondly because the believer remains within history. In principle, the future always offers to man the gift of freedom; Christian faith is the power to grasp this gift. The freedom of man from himself is always realised in the freedom of historical decisions.

The paradox of Christ as the historical Jesus and the

ever-present Lord, and the paradox of the Christian as an eschatological and historical being is excellently described by Erich Frank : '. . . to the Christians the advent of Christ was not an event in that temporal process which we mean by history today. It was an event in the history of salvation, in the realm of eternity, an eschatological moment in which rather this profane history of the world came to its end. And in an analogous way, history comes to its end in the religious experience of any Christian "who is in Christ". In his faith he is already above time and history. For although the advent of Christ is an historical event which happened "once" in the past, it is, at the same time, an eternal event which occurs again and again in the soul of any Christian in whose soul Christ is born, suffers, dies and is raised up to eternal life. In his faith the Christian is a contemporary of Christ, and time and the world's history are overcome. The advent of Christ is an event in the realm of eternity which is incommensurable with historical time. But it is the trial of the Christian that although in the spirit he is above time and world, in the flesh he remains in this world, subject to time ; and the evils of history, in which he is engulfed, go on. . . . But the process of history has gained a new meaning as the pressure and friction operate under which the Christian has to refine his soul and under which, alone, he can fulfil his true destiny. History and the world do not change, but man's attitude to the world changes.'[1]

In the New Testament the eschatological character of the Christian existence is sometimes called 'sonship'. F. Gogarten says : 'Sonship is not something like an habitus or a quality, but it must be grasped ever and again in the decisions of life. For it is that towards which

[1] Erich Frank, *The Role of History in Christian Thought*, pp. 74, 75.

the present temporal history tends, and therefore it happens within this history and nowhere else.' Christian faith just 'by reason of the radical eschatological character of the salvation believed in never takes man out of his concrete worldly existence. On the contrary, faith calls him into it with unique sobriety. . . . For the salvation of man happens only within it and nowhere else.'[1]

We have no time to describe how Reinhold Niebuhr in his stimulating book *Faith and History* (1949) endeavours to explain the relation between faith and history in a similar way. Nor have we time to dispute with H. Butterfield's thought, developed in his book *Christianity and History*. Although I do not think he has clearly seen the problem of historicism and the nature of historicity, his book contains many important statements. And I agree with him when he says: 'Every instant is eschatological'.[2] I would prefer, however, to say: every instant has the possibility of being an eschatological instant and in Christian faith this possibility is realised.

The paradox that Christian existence is at the same time an eschatological unworldly being and an historical being is analogous with the Lutheran statement *simul iustus, simul peccator*. In faith the Christian has the standpoint above history which Jaspers like many others has endeavoured to find, but without losing his historicity. His unworldliness is not a quality, but it may be called *aliena* (foreign), as his righteousness, his *iustitia* is called by Luther *aliena*.

We started our lectures with the question of meaning in history, raised by the problem of historicism. We

---

[1] Friedrich Gogarten, ' Zur Frage nach dem Ursprung des geschichtlichen Denkens' (*Evangel. Theologie*, 1954), p. 232.
[2] *l.c.* p. 121.

have seen that man cannot answer this question as the question of the meaning in history in its totality. For man does not stand outside history. But now we can say : *the meaning in history lies always in the present*, and when the present is conceived as the eschatological present by Christian faith the meaning in history is realised.[1] Man who complains : 'I cannot see meaning in history, and therefore my life, interwoven in history, is meaningless', is to be admonished : do not look around yourself into universal history, you must look into your own personal history. Always in your present lies the meaning in history, and you cannot see it as a spectator, but only in your responsible decisions. In every moment slumbers the possibility of being the eschatological moment. You must awaken it.

[1] Cf. Ernst Fuchs, 'Gesetz, Vernunft und Geschichte' (*Zeitschr. für Theologie und Kirche*, 1954), p. 258.

INDEXES

I. NAMES AND SUBJECTS

II. REFERENCES

Old Testament

<table>
<tr><td colspan="2" align="center">ISAIAH</td><td colspan="2" align="center">DANIEL</td></tr>
<tr><td>xi, 6</td><td>28</td><td>ii</td><td>25, 27</td></tr>
<tr><td>xxiv-xxvii</td><td>21</td><td>vii</td><td>26, 27</td></tr>
<tr><td>xxx, 15</td><td>99</td><td></td><td></td></tr>
</table>

New Testament

MATTHEW		ACTS	
viii, 11	32	iii, 21	26
xii, 45	32	xvii, 30 f.	34
xii, 34	98		

		ROMANS	
MARK		iii, 19	40
		iv, 1-12	34
ii, 18	32	iv, 17	100
viii, 12	32	v, 15	40
viii, 38	32	v, 20 f.	40, 41
ix, 43, 45	32	vi, 12, 14	47
xii, 25	33	vii, 7-25	41
xii, 18-27	32	viii, 12 ff.	46
xiii	33	viii, 23	43
xiii, 32	37	viii, 35-9	43
		ix-xi	42
		x, 4	43
LUKE		xii, 2	46
x, 18	32	xiii, 12	34
x, 23	32	xiv, 7-9	43
		xiv, 17	42

JOHN		I CORINTHIANS	
iii, 18	47	iii, 21-3	43
iii, 19	47	vi, 12	46
v, 24 f.	48	viii, 1-13	46
v, 28	47 n.	ix, 20-2	46
vi, 51-8	47 n.	x, 23-31	46
ix, 39	47	xi, 25	35
xi, 23-6	48	xiii	45
xiv, 2 f.	49	xiii, 12	43
xv, 2-4	48	xv, 24-6	55
xvii, 24	49	xv, 51 f.	33

INDEXES